CRAFT FOR THE SOUL

Pip Lincolne is the author of several
crafty titles (including the bestselling
book *Meet Me At Mike's*.) She is
a mum of three, drinks too much
tea and loves leftovers on toast.

FOR KIRSTY

CRAFT FOR THE SOUL

HOW TO GET THE MOST OUT
OF YOUR CREATIVE LIFE

PIP LINCOLNE

VIKING
an imprint of
PENGUIN BOOKS

FOREWORD BY
CLARE BOWDITCH

Pip and I met online.

I was on tour, missing home, and sitting on the bed in the hotel room looking point-blank at some of the most challenging 'non-original hotel artwork' I'd ever encountered. I'd been reading Pip's blog at the airport that morning and for some reason, on a whim, I decided to share a photo of my #badhotelart with her. We'd never actually met, but her blog was so friendly I felt like I knew her, and for some reason I just figured she'd 'get it'.

When she wrote back with her own picture of #badhotelart I was so delighted that I too replied and then she replied again, and before long a beautiful friendship blossomed.

Every time Pip comes to my house, every interaction I've ever witnessed her having with another human being; these things make her absolutely and perfectly qualified to write a book ON CREATIVITY AND HAPPINESS, because this is what she builds with us, her friends.

The book you're about to read has a lovely cover and a welcoming title, but the truth is it's a wild beast of a thing, this story of CREATIVITY, SIMPLE PLEASURES AND FRIENDLINESS. It's a story of how to cultivate THESE THINGS, and how a little bit of kindness can change the world for the better.

And in a way, it makes Pip Lincolne a little bit of a radical, or so I recently concluded after receiving this precious letter from my friend in the Middle East:

> *I reckon being friendly is almost political. Choosing to be friendly despite the fact that many people are damaged and would rather force their arsehole-ness on the planet is courageous. Friendly is the world I'd rather live in.*

Me too.

Thank you, Pip, for once again illuminating the way for us, and for reminding us of all the little things that make up the kind of world we'd rather live in.

CONTENTS

CHAPTER ONE

Have nice times

NICE TIMES
ARE MY GOAL

I like great times, ace times, rad times, but nice times are generally what I'm aiming for. They're solid and they're warm. Dependable and calm. They're achieved in lots of different ways and aren't quite as frantic as the much more popular happy times.

Don't get me wrong, I'm totally into happiness too. I just think it's become a bit of a buzzword, a commodity, a red herring of sorts. Happiness has become a fairly lofty aspiration and a lot of us are more than a little anxious that we're not measuring up. Gulp.

Happiness is something to celebrate. But don't let it get in the way of you having a nice time: that's so not the point. Happiness anxiety may well be an actual thing. As we're pinning 'Comparison is the thief of joy' quotes to our 'Inspired by' Pinterest boards, we're 'like-ing' photos of perfect apartments in Helsinki and wondering why that's not our life. It's all gone a bit awry.

In her book *The How of Happiness*, Sonja Lyubomirsky writes:

Studies show that 50 per cent of individual differences in happiness are determined by genes, 10 per cent by life circumstances, and 40 per cent by our intentional activities.

She goes on to say that 54 per cent of (US) adults 'lack great enthusiasm for life and are not actively and productively engaged with the world.' And:

> People high in mindfulness – that is, those who are prone to be mindfully attentive to the here and now and keenly aware of their surroundings – are models of flourishing and positive mental health.

Don't you want to be a model of flourishing and positive mental health? I really do. I must have those lucky flourishy genes, because I've learnt to focus and do well despite my circumstances, taking small steps towards goodness, creativity and happiness from an early age. I notice the good stuff that goes on around me. I build opportunities and progress into my day: I'm all about being productive and working on the kinds of projects that are meaningful to me, and I'm into happy moments, as opposed to the high-pressure 'happy life'. I'm narrowing the broad happiness focus to more attainable bite-sized bits. Go me!

This book is a manual on how to do rewarding, bite-sized things, in case you want to shift or refresh your focus too.

Not to put a damper on this positive plan straight away, but we need to talk about the tricky bits, too. Life's really *not* always peachy, is it? Happy's not the default. Crappy stuff does indeed happen and no amount of affirmations can right all wrongs. Illness strikes. Setbacks occur. Depression looms. Insecurity arises. These are the less coveted, very human things life is made of.

I just try to balance these unavoidable annoying bits with plenty of nicer bits. I have systems in place: routines, prompts, guides, things. I've *kind of* worked out how to push right through the tricky stuff. Maybe I can help you to do so, too?

I'm not afraid of the bad bits. Okay, that's a lie. Let's just say I understand that tricky times are an important part of life. As fabulously sparkly and sought-after as HAPPY TIMES are, it's the tricky times that make us who we are. They challenge us and make us dig deep; they make us feel things we haven't felt before and make decisions we didn't know we could. They increase the likelihood we'll get to know ourselves better, and once we see the back of them, they provide contrast and perspective.

I think it's weird that there's this idea that some people have superpowers that attract all kinds of good stuff to them, just by 'asking' for them or through 'positivity'. I know plenty of amazing people who've suffered tough times and setbacks and they certainly didn't manifest them through a lack of positivity. Challenging things happen, even to good people. It's annoying, but true.

In accepting the tough times, I'm not saying you should lower the happiness bar or expect less. I'm suggesting taking a more holistic approach to what matters in life. Expect different kinds of affirming stuff in your life. Happiness matters, but so do all kinds of other great feelings. Nice times are not an all-or-nothing thing, as happiness can be. I've never attracted anything with a superpower, either. There are degrees of goodness we can encourage, though: warmth, cosiness, belonging, progress, productivity. These smaller steps come under the happiness banner and should be appreciated and valued too.

Yes, I want to be happy, but I also want to feel creative, useful, purposeful, appreciated, playful, challenged . . . all kinds of other things. There's a whole bunch of great feelings to be had if we shift the spotlight away from the intoxicating H (happiness). I like the idea of creating nice times and happy moments, with a firm, fortified backbone at the ready for trickier times. That seems more realistic to me. Finding small, practical, simple ways to create a foundation for nice times is what I'm going for.

This doesn't mean that you instantly have a happy life, that the problems you have evaporate, that everything is okay. It does mean that happy moments are yours for the taking, though. Take them when you can. Decide to. Fortify yourself with bite-sized bits of feel-good. Notice the positives. Feel all of the *other good feelings, not just the happy!*

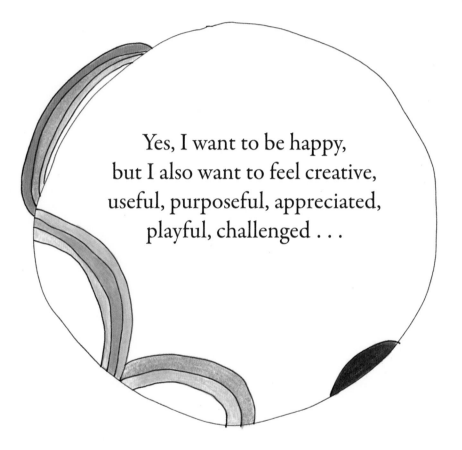

Yes, I want to be happy,
but I also want to feel creative,
useful, purposeful, appreciated,
playful, challenged . . .

WHAT IS HAPPINESS, ANYWAY?

Happiness. Golly. It's a biggie, right? A huge, amazing, helpful industry has sprung up around the happiness ideal. I wasn't sure if this was a recent thing, so I did a bit of digging. Apparently, we only started aiming for happy around the eighteenth century; things have gained momentum since then.

I've been through hard times, as I'm sure you have. Health scares, favourite people dying, pets lost, curve balls thrown. Crappy things have happened to me with alarming frequency. Perhaps you can relate? In these times, I did the sensible thing and turned to . . . self-help books! I read a *lot* of books about happiness, optimism, how we think and what we feel. Lucky for you, this makes me a happiness expert. I've done both practical and theoretical study. I know my way around the happy thing. Here's a bit of what I've learnt.

> Happiness is when what you think, what you say, and what you do are in harmony.
>
> MAHATMA GANDHI

HAPPINESS DEPENDS ON SETTING GOALS

Happiness depends on what you need, where you are now, where you *really* want to be and whether you're taking steps to get there – or at least have a view of the destination.

Difficult stuff, sadness, frustration, anger and ambivalence can be rooted in square-pegging it in a round hole. Doing things you don't want to do with no clear view of where you really want to be will not make you happy. Uh-uh.

If you're living something true to you, on the other hand, you'll feel happier, more creative, more fulfilled. If the decisions you make are based on your own life mission, you'll feel purposeful. If the things that are happening get you closer to the things you hold dear and true, and you're doing things that have meaning to you, you'll feel satisfied.

If it doesn't feel right, then it probably isn't. Your interior barometer will tell you when something's not the best fit for you. Toeing the line, putting up with stuff, enduring: they can be a means to an end goal or signs of a poor fit. Only you know what your truth is. Assess the ill-fitting bits often, and think about whether you need to stick it out or run for the hills.

We can benefit from relaxing into things and going with the flow sometimes. But overall goal-setting is really important. Your goals might be big and loose, like 'Be happy', or they might be smaller, like 'Remember to eat breakfast'. Perhaps they're precise: 'Become a brain surgeon'. Nice. Goals are good.

Creating some clear goals for yourself sets you on a purposeful path. Then, when in doubt, you can refer to your Trusty List'o' Goals and think about whether the things you're up to are getting you closer to these hopes and dreams – and if not, whether it matters. It's good to have a map.

HAPPINESS DEPENDS ON PERSPECTIVE

Sometimes we don't seem to be living the dream. The things we're working on seem menial or boring or not true to us. It's easy to get demoralised when things are moving slowly or not moving at all.

We need to rethink what we're doing. Maybe the stuff we're doing intersects with the seemingly faraway goal we've set ourselves, somewhere along the line. Maybe outcomes are closer than they seem. We need to reframe what we're pushing through and focus on where we're ultimately headed. Creativity, happiness, success. They're not always easy. Sometimes you just have to knuckle down and keep going, trusting the process and assuming the right stuff will happen. That the right things will find you at the right time. They really will. While you are pushing through, you can build in some nice moments and make the most of them. That really helps. Start small.

Anne Lamott's book on writing, *Bird by Bird*, favours this 'get started, keep going, step-by-step' approach. And writing is a great analogy for life. When you're writing a book you *know* you want to write, you have some ideas about how it will go, but in the end you just have to sit down and commit: start typing and see what happens. Often the result is as much of a surprise to the author as it is to the reader. Life can be like that, too.

SILVER LININGS AND GEMS

A while back, a job I worked on seven days a week super-successfully ended suddenly due to budget cuts, and I was left adrift. I quickly got other work to replace the seven-day-a-week passion project, but I was a bit heartbroken and confused by the whole thing. Something I'd put my heart and soul into, something that had done really well and was well-loved and read had just had the pin pulled. A year of committed work had seemingly gone down the drain. I felt sick for two weeks, not putting it down to project grief, but rather thinking I'd been eating too much bread or something. (Why do I blame everything on BREAD? I love bread!)

Anyway, after two weeks, I came out of my fug and felt a whole lot better. And I realised it wasn't the bread after all. I moved on, still confused, but back on my feet and feeling okay. Then it dawned on me. Yes, it was really sad to lose something I loved working on, but working most days on that project had been an amazing learning curve. I'd become *much* better at my work, simply by practising and working hard. And even though I'd left behind the REASON for the hard work, I still had the ethic and skills.

My lost project was a gift, really. It made me a much better writer, publisher and creative. Once I realised this, the weight of loss gave way to the lightness of achievement. It was all about perspective really.

Of course, not all difficult times are as easy to recover from as that. Losing people, pets, houses or health are all much, much worse than my trial. It's hard to find the good in those things, because there often isn't any. BUT. There may be other benefits to those kinds of challenges. A health overhaul. A rekindled relationship. An enforced slowdown. A reality check. Or maybe tinier things: a kind word from someone. A beautiful gift. A bunch of special memories. A fresh new day.

Perspective is vital if you want to stay on track. You can wallow under a blanket and mull over how wronged you've been, or you can work hard at excavating the difficult times to try to find the gems that are hidden within. I vote gems.

ACTIVITIES
Make a list of goals – big and small things
you'd really like to do in this lifetime.

SOME GOAL IDEAS:

→ LIVE IN THE COUNTRY.

→ TAKE A TRIP TO PARIS.

→ TRACE YOUR FAMILY TREE.

→ TRAVEL AROUND AUSTRALIA.

→ BUY A KOMBI.

→ OWN A DACHSHUND.

→ BECOME A DOCTOR.

→ WRITE A BOOK.

→ WORK FOR AN NGO.

→ LIVE TO BE ONE-HUNDRED
AND TEN.

→ BECOME A VEGAN.

→ BUILD A GREAT BUSINESS.

→ BUILD A HOUSE.

→ FALL IN LOVE.

→ LOOK FOR THE LOCH NESS
MONSTER.

→ MEET STEPHEN FRY.

→ RIDE TO THE TOP OF THE
EMPIRE STATE BUILDING.

→ BE SELF-SUFFICIENT.

→ CLIMB A REALLY BIG
MOUNTAIN.

→ RUN A MARATHON.

→ BE ON A GAME SHOW.

→ SEE A WHALE.

→ VOLUNTEER.

→ MAKE ONE MILLION
DOLLARS.

→ ENTERTAIN PEOPLE.

→ WIN AN ESTEEMED PRIZE.

→ GIVE UP SMOKING.

→ STOP BOOZING.

→ SEE THE PYRAMIDS.

→ HAVE CHILDREN.

NICE MOMENTS TO BE MADE:

- → READ A BOOK IN THE QUEUE AT THE AIRPORT.

- → LISTEN TO A PODCAST ON THE BUS.

- → PLAY AN AUDIO BOOK IN THE CAR ON THE WAY TO WORK.

- → USE YOUR WALK TO THE BANK TO THINK ABOUT LIFE'S GOOD STUFF.

- → GET UP AN HOUR EARLIER TO DO SOMETHING YOU LOVE.

- → BUY A GREAT PEN SO THAT YOU CAN WRITE HAPPILY (EVEN IF YOU'RE WRITING BORING STUFF).

- → ALLOW TWICE THE TIME TO DO YOUR WEEKLY FOOD SHOPPING IN A LEISURELY WAY!

- → TAKE YOUR OWN FAVE MAGAZINE TO THE DOCTOR'S WAITING ROOM.

- → WRITE SOMETHING DURING YOUR FLIGHT.

- → WRITE LETTERS TO FRIENDS AND CREATE UNEXPECTED GREAT MOMENTS WHEN YOU RECEIVE A REPLY.

- → WALK YOUR DOG AND NOTICE THE WORLD.

- → GET A REALLY GREAT MUG AND MAKE YOUR TEA-BREAK NICER.

- → MEET A FRIEND FOR LUNCH EACH WEEK.

- → WALK SOME OF THE WAY HOME AND USE THE TIME TO THINK.

- → USE YOUR LUNCH HOUR TO TAKE PHOTOS OR SNIPPETS OF VIDEO.

- → MAKE A DELICIOUS LUNCH FOR YOU.

WHAT MAKES YOU HAPPY?
(as answered by older people)

I asked readers of my blog to chat to the older people in their life, looking for happiness clues. (My mother jokingly responded 'Waking up every day', and my nanna replied, 'Definitely top of the list!')

My grandchildren running up to me and giving me a hug.
MAUREEN: *LANDSDALE, WESTERN AUSTRALIA, 70*

Seeing our family happy and healthy.
PETER & ROBIN: *WOOLLONGONG, NEW SOUTH WALES, 80 & 76*

My children, grandchildren and great-grandchildren make me the happiest and luckiest of all.
SAUL: *TOORAK, VICTORIA, 95*

Seeing all the family sitting around the dining table together.
BARBARA: *BRIGHT, VICTORIA, 75*

Sipping my first cup of tea in the morning and reading the newspaper.
ALICE: *MOUNT LAWLEY, WESTERN AUSTRALIA, 79*

Being alive and able to draw and paint in my newly built outdoor studio overlooking the hills.
DOUGLAS: *MALENY, QUEENSLAND, 84.5*

Spending time with my family and a brandy and dry at the end of the day.
JEAN: *GERALDTON, WESTERN AUSTRALIA, 87*

Gardening and bowls and getting emails from people I care about.
TEX: *NEWCASTLE, NEW SOUTH WALES, 75*

Waking up and feeling well.
BETTY: *PINJARRA, WESTERN AUSTRALIA, 87*

Not just having grandchildren, but playing with them, being silly
and making them laugh.
KEITH: *MELBOURNE, VICTORIA, 75*

When I pick up the phone and hear the words, 'Hi Grandma!'
ANNE: *SYDNEY, NEW SOUTH WALES, 70*

What makes us happy? Need you ask? Our great-grandchildren running up
the drive to see us. Also being in the company of our family. Last night, for
instance. Sorry I can't say parachute jumping or horse riding, but I have to
tell the truth.
BERYL & DAVID: *CARNEGIE, VICTORIA, BOTH 84*

The freedom to make my own decisions.
MARJORY: *YUULONG, VICTORIA, 82*

Raspberry and Coconut Tarts

My nan used to make cakes a bit like these,
and whenever I bite into one I feel like I'm a smock-
frocked four-year-old again . . . in a really good way!

PASTRY	FILLING
50G BUTTER	RASPBERRY JAM
100G PLAIN FLOUR	50G BUTTER
PINCH OF SALT	50G CASTER SUGAR
1TSP CASTER SUGAR	1 EGG, BEATEN
1 EGG YOLK AND COLD WATER TO MIX	50G DESSICATED COCONUT
	3TBSP SELF-RAISING FLOUR

× Pre-heat the oven to 190°C.

× For the pastry, rub the butter into the flour and salt until it resembles breadcrumbs, then stir in the sugar. Make a well in the centre of the mix and pour in the egg yolk and enough cold water to make a firm dough.

× Turn the dough onto a floured board and roll out thinly. Cut into rounds large enough to fill a shallow patty-pan tin. (We use a glass to do this, like Nan used to.) Line each patty-pan hollow, and then put a little bit of jam in each one.

× Now make the filling. Cream the butter and sugar together until fluffy. Add the egg a little at a time, then fold in the coconut and the flour. Place spoonfuls of this mixture on top of the jammy-lined patty pans. It will spread out as you cook it, so don't be too precise.

× Bake for 15–20 mins until golden and firm. Cool and eat!

MAKES ABOUT 12

Cheerfulness, it would appear,
is a matter which depends fully as
much on the state of things within
as on the state of things without
and around us.

CHARLOTTE BRONTË

CHAPTER TWO

Wake up and improve!

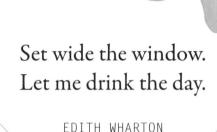

Set wide the window.
Let me drink the day.

EDITH WHARTON

Some people open their eyes in the morning, groan and put the pillow over their head. They are not very zesty. They are cosy-toed. They are not ready to welcome the day.

Maybe they feel like they know what it holds and aren't willing to be part of it. Maybe they're pretending they don't really need that before-work shower today. Maybe they sipped too many drinks-in-a-jar the night before and feel it's not actually possible to roll out of bed. Perhaps the thought of their irritating workmate sprang to mind, prompting a rearranging of blankets and slap of the snooze button. I know how hard the mornings can be. It's quite difficult to get up.

There are other reasons it might be tricky to begin the day. Maybe you're just not a 'morning person'. You might have adorable, naughty, night-waking children who zombify you daily with their foggy-morning magic. Or maybe you just LOVE your bed and want to cosy up under the blankets and drool into your pillow in a snorey-soggy way. Maybe you can NEVER get enough sleep. I get that.

The thing is, even non-morning people have to have mornings. They're just part of life, as sure as night follows day. Or something. Assuming you are not a loll-about-person-of-leisure, the kind who is able to snooze the day away, then there is definitely something in the morning for you.

Mornings. Ah. I love them. They are the key
to productivity, positivity, creativity, activity . . .
all the tivities! Mornings set the tone for the day,
and launching yourself into them with as little
whining as possible will pay big dividends. I think
you can make your mornings SO great that even
the most night-owly types will forgo the drool and
groaning for a bit of perky slipper-shuffling instead.

Or maybe you won't. Maybe you're a stubborn,
mule-y kind. You might want to read this chapter in
a hopeful, aspirational way, KNOWING that you'll
be a morning person one day, if you can just summon
the energy and part yourself from your pondy pillow.

Mornings (especially early mornings) are often
the quietest time of day. This is the perfect time to
make coffee and think about what you need to tackle,
or just sit on the back step and watch everything
slowly get moving. The hardest part is making that
decision to get the heck out of bed. Once you've
done that, you've totally got it nailed. Make a beeline
for the coffee. Flick on the radio. Butter some
crumpets. The day is yours.

START A DAILY MORNING RITUAL

You can develop some good habits that work for you and help you tame your day from the very get-go. Here's how I do it. Maybe you could do what I do, or maybe you have your own bright ideas.

Every day, I wake up as early as possible. That can be any time from 5 am to 6.30 am: the earlier the better, as far as I'm concerned. I'm 100 per cent a morning person. I love going to sleep at night, because I'm already thinking about starting a new day and doing new things and drinking coffee all by myself in the still morning air. I comfy up in bed, close my eyes and happily let the night roll in, because I know it's nearly a new day.

I know. I'm a bit freaky, right? You can call me Pollyanna, but this is how my life works best. Chipper, early mornings get my life off to a good start each day. I sort of wake up and go, 'OKAY!' I try to embrace the day.

Then, to up the freak factor a titch further, I just get up, wipe the night out of my eyes and hurry downstairs to make coffee and think about the things I need and want to do. I can't really be bothered to think of excuses to stay in bed or shorten the nice, quiet early morning. I just get going.

I say hello to my dogs; they jump on my leg with their pointy feet and make me go all wincey. Then I retreat into the kitchen, rubbing my jumped-on legs, and flip on the lights, coffee machine and kettle. I choose a mug, fill it with boiling water to warm it and make a strong-but-milky coffee to start the day. Then I fill my empty water bottle from the tap, maybe make some delicious toast, and wander into the lounge room with the bottle tucked under my arm, mug in one hand, plate in the other.

I turn the heater on, too, in winter. I put the telly on and turn the volume all the way down.

Then I grab a notepad from the bunch that I bought at the newsagent (I like the graph pads with the grids on them, because they help to keep my writing from wigging out too much!), and my fancy pen that my mum gave me. (It's a yellow Lamy one. My mum has every coloured Lamy pen. She's a Lamologist.) And I begin my version of the 'morning pages' from *The Artist's Way* by Julia Cameron.

The Artist's Way suggests writing three longhand pages every day. I am very open to suggestion, possibly to the point where I'd happily join your cult, so I do just that. I write three long, handy, often very messy pages. Comfortingly, Cameron says there is no wrong way to write these pages. They're meant to be a bit of a stream of consciousness. My pages will read something like this:

> Take photos of vintage stamps, walk a mile in my shoes, Furry Friends are so great, ring Gemma, why are there cuticles anyway? blisters suck, don't forget to walk your 10 K, write a poem, the sea, the sea, buy watercolours from Deans Art, remember you're a Womble, get the other Patti Smith bio, Beatrix Potter, cheese, pencil sharpener, Alice B Toklas? Louis Theroux, Louis Theroux, Louis Theroux, bingo!

I know. I am obviously nuts. But after I do this, I feel satisfied. I smooth the pages and look over my 'speed writing' – a kind of hieroglyphics-meets-bonkers-doctor cursive. It's just the look I'm going for. I'm going for it because, apart from being *The Artist's Way*, it's my way. The bonkers pages are part brain-dump, part thought-exorcism and part idea-hatching. They are a no rules, true-to-me confessional, and I like to front up daily with my toast and my fancy pen.

Later, I do the *second* part of my morning ritual. (I am quite the glutton for morning rituals, obviously, because it's my favourite part of the day.) The second part of my morning must-do is to go for a big walk around my neighbourhood. I get dressed (phew!), put on a coat or cardigan, grab my iPhone, headphones and keys. I tuck a notepad and pen in my pocket, shut the door and spring away! Or sometimes I just trudge.

I might walk down my street. Past my favourite cafes, past the bookshop, supermarket, the perfume shop, the florist, the grocer. If I go this way, I walk right to the end of the (very long) street, and then I walk back along the other side.

Usually, though, I go a different way: around the corner, around the park, past the big interesting buildings, past the pond, through the trees, across the muddy bit, past the magnolias, through the grass. That's my preferred route. It's much quieter, and there are trees and flowers and other nature-y things to enjoy. I love a bit of nature in the a.m. It's dewy and fresh.

While I walk, I listen to podcasts and make mental notes about the good things I hear. Sometimes I listen to music if I've run out of podcasts. Sometimes I listen to audio books, making the most of 'reading' time when I'm wandering about. Sometimes, if it's the weekend, I walk back past Babka or lap around to Monsieur Truffe to buy pastries for the people who are still sleeping at my place.

Wincey legs, hot coffee, morning journal pages, walking, ponds and pastry-bestowing are my favourite ways to start the day. You probably didn't know that doing those things could really make your day. Lucky you've got me to clue you in. *wink*

All the bits of these rituals are super-important to me. I know that they might seem like simple little tasks that could easily be pushed aside, but together they conspire to make good stuff happen. These little tasks clear my head, get me focussed, help me think up good ideas and keep me healthy. They fill my lungs with fresh air, my heart with cheer, my brain with thoughts, my muscles with the urge to move. These things help me arrange my day in a positive, practical, creative way. When I don't do them, I feel sluggish and disappointed. When I DO do them, I feel optimistic and productive.

These morning rituals take me about an hour to complete.

If your day isn't home-based and flexible like mine, you could get up a bit earlier and give yourself a sneaky extra half an hour to concentrate on doing things that will ready you for your day. Or, if a mid-morning routine sounds good to you, you could get to work fifteen minutes early and take an extra bit of time on your morning break to even things out.

Find the things that work for you. Giving yourself some time to get energised, inspired and sorted for your day is an excellent idea – and you'll find it also makes you more productive. Magically, just by building in some time for ideas and inspiration and movement, you will gain extra minutes in your day. I don't know how that works, but it really does!

So fine was the morning except for a streak of wind here and there that the sea and sky looked all one fabric, as if sails were stuck high up in the sky, or the clouds had dropped down into the sea.

VIRGINIA WOOLF, *TO THE LIGHTHOUSE*

IMPROVE STUFF

The next thing I try to do each day is IMPROVE something. I am not the sort to plod along, autopiloting through my day in a haze. I'm wide-awake and present (in a non-gift-wrapped way), sorting through the pieces of my life and making sure I like the bits I find.

I'm the type of person who takes stock of my life regularly, too. I like to think about what's working, what's making things tricky and what I can do to make things happier, calmer, easier, nicer, funner, BETTER.

I sort of feel like I should apologise for being so chirpy and do-ey. I am fully aware that such chipper-ness can annoy less perky types. I gather it can grate. But really, it's just the way I am. I'm not doing it to shit anyone. I've just always got an eye on making things better.

I'm not only talking about emotional stuff, either. Improvement comes in many guises. Self-improvement is a good one, yes, but improving things around your house can lead to awesome gains in your life, too. Fixing a torn pocket, replacing a washer, oiling a squeaky hinge, replacing a cracked pane of glass. The benefits of these kinds of small repairs shouldn't be underestimated. Small fixes can spark big reactions.

Jane Ní Dhulchaointigh, inventor of rubbery fixing medium Sugru, discovered this when people started using her product to hack the broken or clunky bits in their lives. Sugru had taken her years to create, perfect and take to market. It moulds to different shapes and then cures to a firm but flexible compound. When Jane launched it with the idea of making things last longer and work better, people not only bought it, they sent her grateful emails explaining how improved their lives were (thanks to her!). Leaky things stopped leaking. Ill-fitting things fitted. Cracks were sealed. These small repairs made a big difference to people's lives. This in turn spurred her on, as she noted, 'People are f*cking awesome'.

Not only did people like Jane's product because it improved annoying bits of their lives, they liked the fact that they could fix things themselves, and that Jane had actually got off her bum and invented something that made stuff work better. It was a kind of irresistible inspiration/improvement/rubbery sandwich.

I think my own fascination with improvement was firmly fixed (pardon the pun) by *Sesame Street*. Thank you Mr Henson. Have you ever watched the early episodes of *Sesame Street*? The show featured, amongst other cool, fluffy, funny things, the Fix-It Shop. The people and puppets of *Sesame Street* would bring their broken bits and bobs to the Fix-It Shop and they'd be repaired in a jiffy by Maria or Luis. There'd be a little life lesson in each improvement, too. Somehow fixing a toaster or blender resulted in new friendships, found pets or happier lives. So powerful, no?!

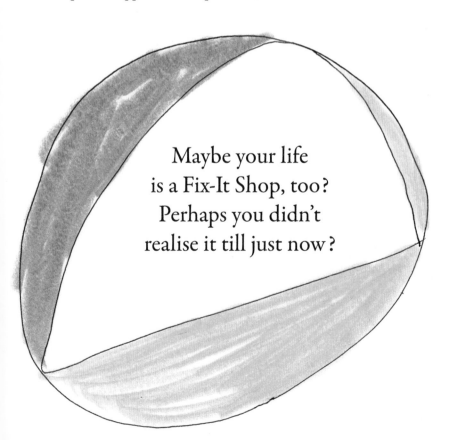

Maybe your life
is a Fix-It Shop, too?
Perhaps you didn't
realise it till just now?

WHAT TO IMPROVE?

Have a think about your life and think about the things you want to fix.
Here are some things I ponder and seek to improve:

→ The dripping tap in the bathroom which makes me lose my MIND every
   time I go to turn it off (after SOMEONE ELSE has left it dripping).
→ The things wrapped in tinfoil floating around the back
   of the fridge. I don't really know what they are.
   Someone else put those there.
→ The post-sushi session drips of soy sauce on our
   coffee table. I don't like soy sauce drips.
→ The fitted sheet. Why does my sheet not want to fit on my bed?
   Does it want to get up?

SOMETIMES IT'S THESE THINGS:
→ Why is my hair a desirable home for small birds?
   Am I a naturalist?
→ Why does white flour make me feel all plumpy?
   Am I intolerant?
→ Why do I insist on putting those cotton buds in my ears when
   I know it's wrong? Am I crazy?

IT MIGHT EVEN BE THESE THINGS:
→ Why am I living in this house when I want to live somewhere else?
→ Why are nannas a bit cross?
→ Why is that annual car registration always a surprise when I drive
   around with the due date on my windscreen?

OR THESE:
→ Why are there always four empty toilet rolls on the floor of the bathroom?
→ Why do leggings seem opaque, when they are in fact a bit showy?
→ Where is my other sock?

Of course, your things, big or small, may be different to these. Your bigs may be bigger. Your smalls may be smaller. Or you might have some crazy cocktail of varied-sized things.

Sometimes, when you look at all the things you want to fix, they form into one big lump. *shudder* The lump seems a bit overwhelming, right? Yes. I'm overwhelmed even TYPING about it. Maybe you are, too? Or maybe not – perhaps you choose not to think about the big lump or the things at all? Maybe you're pushing it away, a bit like the tinfoil-wrapped stuff in the back of the fridge? Waiting for it to make its presence felt when it stinkily chooses? That's probably not a great idea . . . Stinky isn't good.

What we need is action, improvement, focus. We need to drag the lump-forming things out into the bright light of day. I know you KNOW that if you break that big lump of overwhelmingness down into smaller bite-sized pieces, it'll be much easier to tackle. Perhaps you just need someone to tell you to do that? Well, I'm telling you to do it now. Bust out your big lump and break it up. I've made you an awesome Big Lump Excavator. It's a stupid name, I know, but you've got to put a dorky spin on daunting work, I feel. It's on page 28. So put on your overalls and get to work: excavate your big lumps. Write down all of the things. Then make a plan to fix them as best you can.

BIG LUMP EXCAVATOR   POSITIVES

PERSONAL
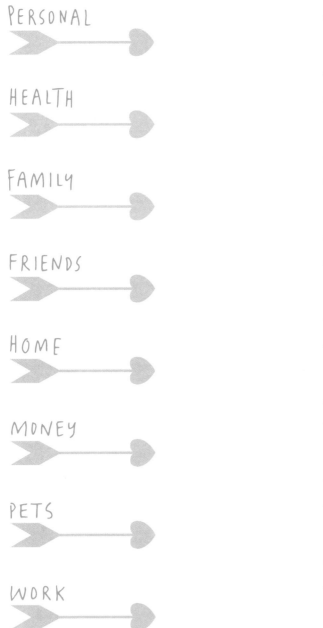

HEALTH

FAMILY

FRIENDS

HOME

MONEY

PETS

WORK

NOTES ON SUCCESS

It's important to track your progress. Once you've started making improvements – setting up fresh and fun routines and changing bits of your life – make sure you take some time to notice the difference they make. Write down the best stuff you're doing and how it affects you positively. Notice whether, when you drop out and stay in bed, that makes you feel restored or kind of sluggish for the day. Do different walking routes have different effects on you? Which bits of the day do you most look forward to now? Which are sucky and need more fixing?

Keeping tabs on what's working is ace, because when you're feeling a bit lost, it gives you a ready-made improvement plan to fall back on. You might be having the crappest day ever, but if you flip through your success notes, you will be faced with a whole heap of things you can do to turn it around. Of course, you may still want to sob quietly under the doona. That's okay . . . Sometimes that's the very best thing you can do.

ACTIVITIES

IDEAS FOR MORNING RITUALS AND ROUTINES:

→ TAKE A WALK.

→ MORNING PAGES.

→ LISTEN TO A FAVOURITE PODCAST OR RADIO SHOW.

→ READ TEN BLOGS YOU LOVE.

→ MAKE A SPECIAL BREAKFAST.

→ WALK YOUR DOG OR SOMEONE ELSE'S.

→ WRITE A POSTCARD AND SEND IT TO A FRIEND.

→ WRITE A POSTCARD AND KEEP IT FOR YOURSELF.

→ TAKE A DAILY PHOTO.

→ READ A CHAPTER OF A FAVOURITE BOOK.

→ GO TO A FAVOURITE CAFÉ.

→ DO SOME YOGA.

→ SIT OUTSIDE IN THE GARDEN OR THE PARK.

→ PHONE A FRIEND.

→ MAKE FRESH JUICE OR A SMOOTHIE.

→ MEDITATE.

→ MAKE SOME BREAD DOUGH TO BAKE LATER.

→ EAT A PASTRY.

→ WRITE IN YOUR JOURNAL.

→ GO FOR A SWIM.

→ PLAY AN INSTRUMENT.

→ SNEAK IN SOME CRAFTING.

→ PICK SOME FLOWERS.

→ WRITE A LIST OF TO-DOS.

→ CATCH UP ON THE NEWS.

BIG LUMP EXCAVATOR (SEE PAGE 28)

Write down parts of your life that might have improvements pending:

Personal
Health
Family
Friends

Home
Money
Pets
Work/Other stuff

START A 'NOTES ON SUCCESS' JOURNAL

Detail the stuff that makes you feel good about life: routines, walks, smells, people, places, food, that kinda thing.
Turn to this in tough times.

My Favourite Pancakes

Pancakes always seem to come out better if you leave the batter to sit for a while. When I'm really organised, I leave it overnight. If you can't be bothered to do that, it's okay, though. Just batter up in your slippers and cook them straight away. They'll be delicious no matter what!

2 CUPS OF SELF-RAISING FLOUR

½ CUP OF CASTER SUGAR

1 TSP BAKING POWDER

1 EGG

2 CUPS OF MILK

1 TSP VANILLA EXTRACT

BUTTER FOR THE PAN
(50G SHOULD DO IT)

× Sift the dry ingredients together and make a well in the centre. Beat the egg and milk and vanilla together. Add the wet ingredients to the dry and whisk until everything is combined. You don't need to mix it any more than that.

× Heat a heavy-based pan over a medium heat. Add a knob of butter, and once it's melted and coated the pan, spoon in a generous tablespoon (and a bit extra!) of your batter. (I use a pastry brush to brush the butter all over the pan to be double-sure nothing sticks.)

× Cook until lots of bubbles appear on the uncooked side – maybe 3 minutes? Add an extra sliver of butter to the pan. Once the butter has melted, flip your pancake and cook for another 3 minutes or so on the other side. You want that batter to puff up and cook through beautifully, so be patient.

× Remove the cooked pancake and keep it warm under foil. Keep spooning and flipping until you've used all the batter.

MAKES ABOUT 10

CHAPTER THREE

Movement is the key to happiness and creativity

HERE'S WHY
YOU SHOULD WALK

A lot of people view exercise as the pursuit of the fit, firm or facile. I don't think there's anything superficial about wanting to be fit and firm, but I understand that the Sporty And Hot movement can marginalise those who don't feel they are sporty and/or hot, to say the least.

Exercise can seem like the domain of nuggetty-armed dudes and camel-toed ladies, but there's more to it than that. Firstly, if nugget arms make you feel good, then go for it. Secondly, if you have lady bits, you might have a camel toe sometimes. Deal with it peeps, it's just anatomy! But we weren't really talking about intimate anatomy . . . or WERE we?! Let's move on.

Movement is not just for the sporty. Movement is for the non-sporty too. Movement is for everyone. Activity and movement are the keys to happiness and creativity. If the Sporty And Hot idea of moving has you hiding out on the couch at home mumbling, 'I'm not that kind of person', think again. You, my friend, are hiding from happiness. Not only that, you are hiding from creativity, ideas, inspiration, joy, play, sleep, love, health and productivity. Why are you doing that?

Let me explain.

I used to think of walking as 'my exercise'. I had it all tied up with the task of completing 10 000 steps a day. I was trying to increase my fitness, lung capacity and muscle strength. I was trying to do the best thing for my body and create a healthy habit. I'd struggled with all kinds of asthma and chesty issues all my life, so I needed to do something. Walking was that thing. I'd think about the correct runners, the correct music to walk to, the right sporty clothes, the water bottle, the equipment, the time, all of the THINGS. It was quite overwhelming and seemed like an epic amount of preparation for something I deemed SPORTY and not that interesting.

It was only when I stopped thinking of walking as something I was doing to increase my physical fitness that I began to notice all sorts of gains. Not only did I stop worrying about *all of the things*, just putting on comfy shoes and a coat to get started (plus OTHER clothes, don't freak out!), I realised that the act of getting out and about in the fresh air – looking at my neighbourhood and the people walking by and the trees and flowers and grass – was about a lot more than keeping my body in good working order. It was a wake-up walk in all kinds of ways.

Walking about, being outside, committing to time away from work and home gave me a huge boost in the happiness and creativity stakes. Here's why you should walk this way.

An early-morning walk is a blessing for the whole day.

HENRY DAVID THOREAU, *WALDEN*

REASONS TO
TAKE A WALK

1. WE NEED NATURAL LIGHT

I recently read an article on the Smithsonian website that talked about early rising. As you know, I'm really interested in waking up early and its benefits, so I read on with interest.

The writer explained that late risers who were sent on week-long camping trips were exposed to more natural light than their stay-at-home buddies. Their natural circadian rhythms (the daily cycles of living things) adjusted to the increased light by returning to the body's default 24-hour cycle. This 'reboot' of the campers' systems meant they began to release the sleep-inducing hormone melatonin at sunset and reduce its production at sunrise, as humans are meant to. This led to sounder sleep, earlier nights and earlier mornings too.

This is how we're all supposed to live, ideally, but the ambient light from all the screens we operate with and lights we live under has tweaked our natural rhythms and convinced some of us that we're not meant to be morning people. This is so not true.

These studies show that even the most diehard night owl can shake up their routine and drink in the beauty of the early morning, if they so choose. Apart from restoring your circadian rhythm, being out in the sunshiney day will expose you to a restorative dose of vitamin D, which increases production of the happy hormone seratonin, helps our muscles function better and even activates appetite-suppressing leptin. Thinner, earlier, happier. What could be better than that?!

2. WE NEED FRESH AIR

Being stuck inside means we are living out many hours of the day possibly exposed to all kinds of BAD indoorsy things. Chemicals and irritants via air-conditioning, cleaning products and tiny, floaty bits from building materials; bugs like colds and flu being piped through ventilation systems. These are the mini-environments many of us exist in for the bulk of our week. *shudder*

What we need is fresh air. A Berkeley Lab study of classroom absences showed that just by opening classroom windows and letting the fresh air in, illness and absences were reduced. Lots of the classrooms were ventilated at way under the required level for up to 95 per cent of the time, possibly a lot like our working environments. It seemed like a great idea to save on heating and cooling costs by keeping classrooms shut up tight, yet the savings on non-attendance-related costs like childcare and healthcare, once they opened windows and let the fresh air in, ran into the hundreds of millions. It's almost definitely the same for a lot of workplaces.

It seems like *such* a simple thing to bring fresh air into our day. I don't even need to do a study to know that fresh is best and that humans need to breathe nice, outdoorsy, non-air-conditioned, non-germy, non-chemically air. I am a genius, no? Take my advice and try air.

3. WE NEED A CHANGE OF SCENERY AND ROUTINE

We need to shake things up. We need to be open to new things. As great as the place where we spend our day might be, it can put a damper on inspiration and joy. Getting outside and going for a walk exposes us to new people, new imagery, new smells, sounds, colours, places. It's impossible to know what may pop up in our path – what opportunities or ideas might present themselves – unless we move out of the spot we're in at least SOME of the time.

In Augusten Burrough's very great book *This is How* (in the chapter 'How to find love'), he talks about a 2010 *Science* magazine study that analysed mobile phone data. The study showed that most people 'seemed to stick to the same small area, a radius of six miles or less'. Augusten goes on to say that if you want to find love, you need to 'get out of your own way' and change your patterns. Treading the same old boards will not help you get fresh, somewhere fresh with someone fresh. (Obviously I am not looking for love, because I walk the same park each day, every day. My boyfriend WILL be pleased.)

The point is, that if you want a different result, a different idea, a different feeling, a different life, you need to do something different.

I'm not promising you that walking will help you find love. But the thing is, it might. Or it might help you find good ideas or interesting places you want to go. It will certainly do a heck of a lot more than sitting in a chair, at your desk, looking into a bit-too-cold cup of coffee will. Get up and out of your own way. Listen to Augusten and me. See where it takes you.

4. WE NEED TO COMMIT TO DOWNTIME AND MAKE ROOM FOR IDEAS

We're all super-scheduled, super-plugged-in, super-informed, to-do-listed up. We're trying to make the most of every minute, choose between single-tasking and multi-tasking, get results, learn stuff, be focussed and work diligently. We're trying to do our best and perform optimally. It's kind of exciting and kind of exhausting. Sometimes progress is slow. Often we get so caught up in our tasks and obligations, trying to prioritise and finalise, that we end up being really unproductive or going through the motions or just feeling overwhelmed. Gah.

Downtime is the cure. This quiet time out, this creative pause, is the very thing you need to reboot your day, catch your breath and foster good ideas. It doesn't have to mean you do nothing. It can mean you set off with nothing but the thought that you might feel the happy glow that a calm life brings. Or that you might think of something good. Or notice a thing you haven't seen before. It's all about making room for goodness. Good ideas. Good feelings. Good experiences. Very often, solutions to problems spontaneously spring to mind, conflicts seem less important and perspective washes over everything in a really sensible way. Downtime has these superpowers.

A daily walk is a simple way to create downtime. You make the rules. Perhaps you want to leave your phone at home and walk unplugged to make room for your thoughts. Maybe you want to take your phone and listen to a podcast to spark fresh ideas. Will music help you switch out of your usual routine and transport you to another world?

Maybe you just want to walk quietly without distractions. University of California's Professor Jonathan Schooler suggests:

> If you are stumped, take a break. Allow the unconscious processes to take hold. But rather than just sitting there, you might want to take a walk or a shower or do something like gardening.
>
> 'Five ways to be creative' on BBC Science

Science says these kinds of passive tasks can help trigger creative brainwaves. Commit to this downtime often and let your mind wander, if you can. See how it works for you.

When I walk, as I mentioned before, I like to listen to interesting people on my phone via podcasts and audio books. I've learnt to take a tiny notepad and pen and stop often to write things – ideas, points, words – down in it. Then when I get home I expand on these ideas, working out where they fit into my life (if I can read my own writing!). Maybe this would work for you too? Do that if that seems right for you. Experiment and find your own downtime approach.

5. WE NEED TO GET OUR BLOOD PUMPING AND STRETCH OUR MUSCLES

I guess this IS a fitness thing. Walking promotes heart and lung health. It reduces the risk of diabetes, heart disease and stroke. It promotes good circulation and prevents joint pain and stiffness. It makes us stronger, helps us lose weight, promotes good mental health – and that's just for starters.

If we want to be happy and healthy, we've got to take ourselves out for a spin, be part of the world as often as possible. I'm an all or nothing gal, so a daily habit is perfect for me. On the days that I don't manage a walk for one reason or another, I notice a big difference in how I feel mentally and physically. I feel tired, negative, heavy and teary even. A walk a day fixes all that. Whodathunkit?!

6. WE NEED TO NOTICE OTHER PEOPLE AND FEEL THAT WE BELONG

It's easy to live in your own little world. You have your ace friends. You have your workmates. You might have kids or people you see at school. Perhaps you've got a nice lady that sells you a loaf of bread a couple of times a week. Maybe a man that weighs your apples and gives you a free cheesy cracker at the grocery shop. You know these people. They are solid and comforting. They are regular players in your own theatre of life.

The good news is, there are other people you should know about. Some of them you might get to know. Others you might view from afar as they weave in and out of your day. When you make the time to leave your house or work or place of study, you see all kinds of people you might not otherwise know about. People wearing parkas walking their naughty dogs. People pushing trolleys full of things in plastic bags. People playing violins in front of open violin cases. People throwing bread at fluttering birds. People riding skateboards, pushing prams, scooting by.

There are stories, faces, lives all around you. Taking the time to notice them, to wonder, to steal glances or overhear conversations helps you find your own place amongst them.

Today, on my walk, for instance, I saw a man with his feet planted firmly in the dewy grass, camera to eye, in front of a row of camellia bushes. He was concentrating hard, taking photos of the blooms, trying different angles, adjusting his settings. It made me smile, because he was on a creative mission, noticing something beautiful, documenting it earnestly, ignoring the fact that it was a freezing cold Sunday morning when most people would rather be tucked up in bed with a croissant and a cup of tea.

I felt like we were part of some secret gang. Both adjusting our settings in different ways. We never spoke. He didn't even notice me, he was being so flowery. But the fact that we were both out in the cool morning air, on a dedicated quest for happiness, goodness, learning and inspiration made me feel like I belonged. That there are lots of people like me about the place. That we're all a team. That others care about the kinds of things I do. That I am part of something. And that I took the time to notice that. You should do that too.

If you want good things to happen, if you want different things to happen, if you want sweetness, cleverness, happiness . . . interesting-ness in your life, you must decide to go and find it.

Plan your own daily wake-up walks. I promise it will change your life in all kinds of great ways.

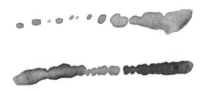

HOW I
GOT A BIT
HEALTHIER

For me, my health and wellness is linked to my emotional state pretty closely. When things are a bit spiralling-out-of-control, chances are my diet, exercise and creative practices are whizzing about unkindly too. Actually, that's the way I used to be.

Now, I'm not like that. I know that looking after yourself is the only way you can live a happy life. So look after myself I do. (Most of the time. Except for when I eat the pick 'n' mix.)

Many of us are quite enamoured with the idea of changing our shape. We are too big or too small or too squishy or too wide. We're also worried about what we're eating. Some of us have it totally nailed and are carefully placing just the right foods into our mouths. Others swing wildly between 'all of the cheeses' and 'I'm on the Neanderthal diet. I only eat Jurassic greens and sushi-ed fish-with-feet'.

I'm totally against fad diets, health crazes, timed health goals (lose five kilos in five weeks, etc.) and scales. I'm all for a much broader, holistic, long-term approach. I think you should be like that too. Sorry to be bossy and all, but adjusting your health habits for the long term will pay long-term dividends. It will change your life. Those short-term approaches will change your month, maybe even your week. Then they'll set you on the path to wrack and ruin, as their tricky, torturous goals are impossible to maintain.

I'm all for the 'gaining health' approach. I think you need to treat yourself nice and change your life. Here's how I got healthier over a period of twelve months, with no real end-goal apart from being strong and healthy. Along the way I lost fifteen kilos, but I learnt that this is not so much about weight loss as health optimisation. When I stuck to my healthy habits, I didn't have to work too hard at losing weight, and I gained a lot of muscle too. Plus, I hardly ever got sick. And I felt like I was being a pal to myself.

1. ACCOUNTABILITY

I started a Facebook group for reluctant exercisers. I hated exercising and I had every excuse in the book *not* to. I knew that if I made some kind of a commitment, though, not only to myself but to other people, I would have a much better chance of success. This group is amazing. We talk about body image, exercise equipment, work-outs and feminism. It's totes diverse, non?

2. EXERCISE PROGRAM

I hired a cross-trainer. That's a fancy piece of equipment that makes your arms and legs swoosh about at the same time. In the beginning, I could only do thirty seconds at a time before my heart wanted to explode and my lungs burnt like a forgotten marshmallow. I worked up to ten, then fifteen, then twenty minutes. And then I took the plunge and started the Couch to 5K program (but on the cross-trainer, because it was the most convenient to my couch). This eventually led to forty-minute sessions, increased fitness and being HEAPS stronger too. Setting a program is a great idea, methinks. One year on, and I'm still swooshing about on it really regularly.

3. FOOD

I ate lots of great homemade things, but I ate too much white flour, rice, bread and pasta. I switched those out for smaller amounts of unprocessed grains (brown rice, seedy bread, wholemeal flour) and I noticed I felt MUCH more energetic and strong and virtuous. I also started snacking on healthy things more often and ate tonnes of salads and healthy soups. Putting all that good stuff into my body made me feel great.

4. BOOZE AND SUGAR

Don't have them. There are lots of books and movements to help you wean yourself off alcohol and sugar: use them if it helps. I just decided to stop having booze and sugar as a habit. I cut out alcohol for the long term, and after eliminating sugar for about four months, I kind of lost the taste for it and only have it occasionally. I feel much better for it – mindful, calm and kind to myself. These are all good things. Sometimes I have chocolate. No biggie. (It does make me jump about a bit, though.)

5. SELF-ASSESSMENT

I have a good talk to myself every week or so to see how I'm going. If I'm noticing that I'm feeling tired or feeling like eating a whole world of golden fried things every day (as opposed to some of the time), then I have a little bit of a heart to heart with myself. Usually there's something else lurking about making me feel anxious or insecure, and I'm channelling that into all kinds of sluggish, slothy habits. Once I remind myself that I'm being a bit of a bully-to-me I get back on track and sort myself out. It's important to call me out on bad behaviour, I think!

WHY WALKS ARE RAD

Natural light
Fresh air
Change of scenery
Downtime
Body health
Noticing people and things

Pip's Really Very Best Cauliflower Salad

1 SMALL CAULIFLOWER, CUT INTO SMALL PIECES

1 HANDFUL OF SNOW PEA SPROUTS

1 CUPS OF COOKED BROWN RICE (WARMED UP SO IT'S SOFT)

1 CUP OF CORN KERNELS (COOKED FRESH ONES OR CANNED)

A TINY BIT OF CHILLI POWDER (NOT TOO MUCH!)

1 TSP CORIANDER

½ TSP CUMIN

SALT AND PEPPER

A GOOD SLOSH OF OLIVE OIL

1 LEMON

SOME FRESH HERBS (PARSLEY OR MINT!)

A HANDFUL OF ALMONDS OR WALNUTS

¼ CUP OF NICE GREEK YOGHURT

A CUPPLA SPOONFULS OF KASUNDI OR SPICY TOMATO/CHILLI TYPE RELISH

×   Pile the cauliflower onto a baking tray and add the olive oil, cumin, coriander and some salt and pepper. Toss well and roast for 15 minutes in a 400 degree oven.

×   On a serving platter (or in individual bowls): tumble the snow pea shoots. Tip the brown rice on top, making it all look nice and rustic and well spread out, messy style. Add the corn on top of that, spread it about with love.

×   Pile the now-cooked cauliflower on top of that, how good does it look?!

×   Plonk a couple of spoonfuls of Kasundi or other spicy chutney/sauce on top.

×   Now plonk a couple of spoonfuls of yoghurt on too. Season with salt and pepper.

×   Scatter with fresh herbs and nuts.

×   Add a squeeze of lime.

×   Eat it up!

×   Variation: Add grilled chicken or tofu for extra oomph!

SERVES 4 PEOPLE OR 2 REALLY HUNGRY PEOPLE

TOP TIPS FOR PERSONAL HEALTH

Be accountable
Have an exercise program
Eat good food
Reduce booze and sugar
Self-assess

ACTIVITIES

Make a list of good places to walk in your town.

Start your own online exercise group – or one in real life where you can meet up and walk together.

CHAPTER FOUR

Be yourself

WHO ARE YOU?

A big part of having a nice life is working out what's important to you. Who are you? What's meaningful to you? What kinds of themes frequently pop up in your life? Who do you look up to? When and where are you happiest? How do you feel a lot of the time? What's your story?

I've been thinking about this a lot recently. I really feel that when you cosy up and get to know yourself, things fall into place more easily. Life is better. Everything has a clarity to it and things feel more purposeful and sure.

I've written a bunch of exercises in this chapter to get you started on getting to know yourself. For this little meet-and-greet, you'll need a notebook and some time. Don't try to do all the exercises at once, though: try for no more than one a day. It's quite hard to summarise who you are, especially when you're caught up in a busy life, fishing socks from down the back of the washing machine or trying to stay out of the armpit of that close-standing man on the bus. Pace it as you need to.

Are you super crazy busy? Does the idea of finding time to do these things for/about yourself seem about as achievable as finishing a thousand-piece puzzle of a Middle Ages market scene? (I tried that. It's definitely NOT achievable, making it an outstanding metaphor.) My advice to you is either a) get up half an hour earlier and devote some time to you, or b) forget about doing the dishes/vacuuming/underpant-ironing here and there and invest in some self-maintenance instead. No one will know that your seams aren't pressed or that there are chicken nugget crumbs under the coffee table. They will, however, notice how glowing and self-aware you've become and want to share in your shininess.

WRITE YOUR TEN-LINE SUMMARY OF YOU

Write ten lines about you: your personality, what you're like, what's at the heart of you. You don't have to show anyone; it's just a way of stepping back and checking the view. Mine goes a bit like this.

TEN-LINE SUMMARY OF ME

I love writing, publishing, making things, having ideas.

I am sentimental, sensitive, silly and nostalgic.

I am hard-working, motivated and tenacious.

I am obsessed with learning, improving and being productive.

I try hard to do a great job at most things.

I'm motivated to work hard and aim for success because I want my kids to be proud of me and know the value of perseverance and hard work.

The things I make and create have links to my childhood or they seek to create joy.

I prefer collaboration to competition.

I want to work until I am eighty or more, because I love new projects and being useful.

Every day I try to think of good ideas, create good things and/or learn from good people.

When you're feeling a bit hazy or lost, read over your ten lines. Remember who you are, what you're made of, what's at the heart of what you do.

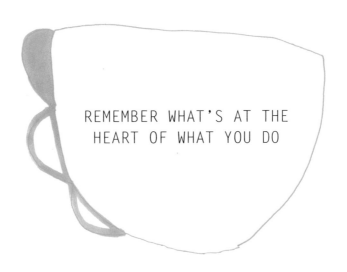

REMEMBER WHAT'S AT THE
HEART OF WHAT YOU DO

WRITE YOUR MISSION STATEMENT

The next part of your story is about what you want to do. What are you trying to achieve? What are the broad goals that define your path? This activity isn't meant to be specific: it's more about putting your finger on the basic structure that gives meaning to your life. (More specific goals fit in UNDER these broad life-pillars.)

Now write your own mission statement. This statement is less about your own personality and more about what you want to achieve with your work or actions. My mission statement looks like this. (Yours will be different to this, probably!)

MY MISSION STATEMENT

→ HAVE AN INTERESTING LIFE.

→ NURTURE CREATIVITY.

→ INSPIRE HAPPINESS AND PLAYFULNESS.

→ CONTRIBUTE TO THE COMMUNITY.

→ MAKE FRIENDS.

→ HELP OTHER PEOPLE MAKE FRIENDS TOO.

WRITE YOUR LIFE RULES

Now think about how you want to live. If you had to write a set
of rules for your life, ten or twelve basic guidelines that helped you
steer your day, what would they be?

MY LIFE RULES

- → PRIORITISE HEALTH.

- → PRIORITISE TIME ALONE.

- → BE MINDFUL AND SEE PLENTY
  OF FRIENDS AND FAMILY.

- → PRIORITISE CREATIVITY.

- → KNOW MY OWN STORY.

- → IMPROVE SOMETHING
  EVERY DAY.

- → TRY NEW THINGS.

- → LOOK FOR CLUES AND SIGNS.

- → EMBRACE WORK.

- → CELEBRATE HAPPY MOMENTS.

WRITE YOUR BIOGRAPHY

And finally, look back. Write your own bio. Write a page or two about
you, so far . . .

- → TALK ABOUT YOUR CHILDHOOD,
  WHERE YOU WERE RAISED,
  WHAT IT WAS LIKE, YOUR
  FAMILY, YOUR PETS, YOUR
  HOME, YOUR SCHOOL.

- → WRITE ABOUT SOME OF THE
  GOOD THINGS YOU DID THEN,
  WHAT MADE YOU HAPPY,
  MEMORIES YOU MIGHT HAVE,
  HOLIDAYS, FRIENDS.

- → WRITE ABOUT GROWING UP
  AND STUDYING OR YOUR FIRST
  JOB. WHAT WORK DID YOU
  DO AND WHERE?

- → WRITE ABOUT WHEN YOU MOVED
  OUT OF HOME: WHAT WAS IT
  LIKE, WHERE DID YOU LIVE?

- → WHAT OTHER JOBS DID YOU
  HAVE, BACK THEN?

- → HAVE YOU TRAVELLED?
  WHERE TO?

- → WRITE ABOUT YOUR FRIENDS,
  PARTNERS AND FAMILY NOW.

- → WHERE DO YOU LIVE NOW?

- → WHAT ARE THE GOOD THINGS
  YOU'RE DOING NOW?

- → WHAT ARE YOU MOST PROUD OF?

- → WHAT IS LIFE LIKE NOW?

- → WHAT ARE YOUR HOPES FOR
  THE FUTURE?

BE PROUD
OF WHO YOU ARE

Let's do a simple test: Are you constantly ticking boxes marked 'new skill', 'new experience' or 'new me'? Do you have a mental list of things you need to do/be, to be the proper version of you? Have you forgotten about all the good things you achieved last year? If you answered 'yes' to two or more of these questions, come and sit by me.

I think this is a case of being hung up on an idea of legitimacy that doesn't really exist. And I think this idea of legitimacy can hold us back.

Yes, it's really great to be improving, learning, pushing forward to new goals all the time. But NO, don't do it without thinking about where you've been and what you've already achieved. Don't rest on your laurels. They're not comfy. But DO notice and honour your progress so far. (And don't let reaching for the new stop you from mastering the old, either.)

Take stock, instead of measuring and constantly looking ahead. Muse back on your (mostly, I'm sure) rad life. If you take the time to think about where you are and how you got there, if you take stock of how well you've done to get to this bit (and the crappy bits you managed to navigate), then you're forging onward to further improvements with a really firm, grounded, realistic, kind footing.

Focus on the good as often as you can. Make it your good habit.

GETTING STUCK

Sometimes we get stuck. We want to be doing good stuff, but we're in a bit of a holding pattern. We're on autopilot. We're unthinkingly sticking to a script that keeps us feeling comfy and ensures we stand a chance of knowing what will happen next.

Sometimes the script was taught to us by our mum or dad or grandparents. We slot in, chattering out dialogue that's more about our history than what we *want* to say. We're talking our family language, and responding in ways that seem familiar but are possibly not really true to us.

It's important to challenge the patterns we're stuck in. If you had a dad who was hilariously sarcastic, you might put a snarky spin on life too. Perhaps your mum was a bit of a Negative Nancy. You probably catch yourself thinking like that as well. It's totally infuriating when we pick up our parents' bad habits, but it's totally fixable if we're vigilant and can catch ourselves doing it.

(Mum. If you are reading this, I am not talking about you. It's a hypothetical example. As you were. Smooches.)

Sometimes, to be who we are and tell our own story, we've got to be more mindful of our default. If you don't want to be a Negative Nancy (and really, who would want that?), then you've got to have words with yourself when you do. Give your NN mum[*] a respectful nod as you walk away from Our Lady of Pessimism. There are probably a tonne of great things/skills/patterns you inherited from family members. Celebrate those and cut the chaff from the wheat, peeps.

[*] Mum, I super-promise it's not you!

LEGIT VS FRAUD

I have a theory that we're all seeking legitimacy. It's a big part of what drives us – we all need to feel deserving of and comfortable with our accomplishments, titles or roles. If we call ourselves a writer, we want to be the BEST kind of writer. If we're learning to paint, we want to do it REALLY well. We want to be the best teacher or parent or marketer or blogger. We want to do well, earn our stripes, study in earnest and be recognised and revered by peers for our success and skill.

Sadly, we often couple this with a dose of Imposter Syndrome, a snarky hurdle that's completely at odds with celebrating achievements and our urge to persevere.

I didn't actually know much about Imposter Syndrome until recently. (I was too busy trying to keep my Improver Syndrome under control.) Luckily, my friend Kirsty explained it to me. Now I can explain it to you.

Imposter Syndrome pertains to feeling like a fraud (or an undeserving imposter), even when you've accomplished your goals though hard work and dedication. Imposter Syndrome sufferers believe the success they've achieved is not deserved – that it should happen to a different kind of person. That they're not of the calibre that can carry this kind of success. That they're destined to be found out, to make a mistake. That people will soon realise that they're a fraud (they are NOT!), and that they're not very interesting, talented or worthy of attention. That the thing they did was not actually as good as it first seemed. Ugh.

The achievement may not feel the way they thought it would, or they may not look the way an achiever 'should'. Sometimes Imposter Syndrome shows itself as a nasty voice, self-talking us into submission, making us doubt ourselves and shut down or give up. Does this sound familiar to you?

I get this sometimes, like if I have to appear on TV or speak in front of a large group of people. I kind of think, 'Oh my god. I need to put on some armour. I need to have the right hair and the right outfit and the right FONT IN MY PRESENTATION SLIDES! I need to look like the person they think I am! What does that person look like? Oh my god!' *googles* 'Oh gosh, do I look like that?! Gulp!'

I then feel *sure* that they've asked the wrong person along, because, well, um, ME. Next, I become a bit obsessed with LOOKING like the right person: having the correct shoes, trying to defrag the cowlick in my fringe, and plucking my eyebrows into stylish, artisan shapes. After that, I step it up in terms of the work I'll deliver to these people who are thinking the things about me that might be better than the things I am. You'll find me attempting to create the world's most insanely interesting/useful/easy/funny/cute/beautiful project, or taking humorous props along so that people won't notice it's me.

These things do not help.

What DOES help is taking a long, hard look at yourself from someone else's admiring point of view. And I do mean someone else's. Under no circumstances listen to your own insecure, worried, self-talking self. That bit of you is probably not your ideal wingman or winglady right now. That self-talk says nuts stuff. For instance, when it talks to me, I hear myself pointing out my (alleged) Bert Newton cheeks or my inadequate eyelashes. Sometimes, I hear me say stuff about my complete lack of professional polish or my annoyingly quirky style. One time I heard me say that I was irritatingly cheery and didn't know how to apply blusher properly. Gah. Luckily, no one else can hear this stuff. If they could, they'd probably want to slap me and send me to my room.

What's with us, huh? We're pushing for legitimacy, to be a success. But when we get there we're looking over our shoulder and mumbling, 'Success? Who, me?' Bonkers. And it's not just me... Leo Babauta of the blog Zen Habits wrote about handling Imposter Syndrome like this:

> I try to be myself, which is really the best I can do. If I'm authentic, I can't be a fraud, because I'm just being who I am. Of course, I'm always trying to figure out who that self is, and the self is constantly changing, so it's an interesting endeavour.

→ Super-fave Tavi Gevinson spoke about it at the Melbourne Writers Festival, saying she felt inauthentic trying to be authentic sometimes.

→ Meryl Streep says, 'Put blinders on to those things that conspire to hold you back, especially the ones in your own head.'

→ Emma Watson: 'Any moment, someone's going to find out I'm a total fraud, and that I don't deserve any of what I've achieved.'

→ Jodie Foster: 'I always feel like something of an impostor. I don't know what I'm doing . . . I suppose that's my one little secret, the secret of my success.'

I've talked to a lot of less famous creative people in my life about this paradox too, and they nod madly when I mention the idea of success being tied in with feeling undeserving.

Be yourself; everyone else is already taken.

OSCAR WILDE

WHAT'S THIS ALL ABOUT?

→ Is this about comparison? About thinking, 'Who are WE to think we can do/try/achieve/say/think (insert thing)?' Are we qualified? Are we an expert? Are we cute enough? Don't we need to know/do/learn/be more? Isn't there someone better/younger/ smarter/more experienced for this job/thing?

→ Is it about confidence? Thinking we're actually really not the sort of person who deserves great stuff? That we're much better suited to being a bit player, less of the lead role in the school play and more of the tree or the cloud, perhaps?

→ Is it about safety? Is it easier to be the tree? After all, it's less scary: we're still part of the production but don't have the pressure of lines and cues. Are we telling ourselves we're not worthy because we secretly don't want to back ourselves?

→ Is it about comfort, maybe? Is it quite nice to be in a holding pattern? Does movement forward feel risky and unnerving? Are we more comfy staying put? Maybe we're a bit lazy, even? Is it all a bit much?

→ All the great things about learning, improving, seeking success and feeling legitimate are undone by the Imposter. We need to cut that dude loose. Open the door to him and you open yourself up to a futile whirlwind of insecurity, inaction and indecision. This gets you nowhere. It also cheats you of experiences, ideas, successes, wins. We need to leave all that crapola at the door, accept what we're achieving, pat ourselves on the back and embrace the wonderful things we're doing.

THE LENS OF DYSFUNCTION

I have a theory that we all get a bit obsessed with dwelling on the past, talking about the crap bits in life, assessing our 'issues' and applying them to everything we do like a liberal dose of calamine lotion on an itchy mosquito bite. You know as well as I do that calamine lotion is not going to fix that itch. It might help for a little while, but before you know it you'll have pinky, chalky bits under your nails and a bunch of scratch marks.

I think our love of telling stories about overcoming obstacles has spun things on their head a little. We love to hear about people who've escaped poverty or dysfunction or difficulty and gone on to achieve success. But as much as the difficulties can be a motivator, they don't define that person, though they might create that first itch. It's good to reflect on the obstacles and hardship, but it's also really important to notice the hard work, tenacity, perseverance and skill that succeeder has used to pull the positive from the equation and let it see the light of day.

Some people achieve great stuff by fronting up, getting started and pushing through. Others are still sitting in their lounge room talking about how they wished they'd gone to school for longer or grown up in a bigger city, or that their grandfather wasn't a crazy booze-hound, or that they hadn't had to change schools so many times, or that they'd had a more present dad, that they'd had better health or been breastfed for longer, blah blah blah. Sorry.

I'm not saying these are not important, significant things to live through, worry about or ponder. What I am saying is that while those things are part of you, they are not who you are. They don't need to hold you back. You don't need to write a disclaimer about why you're not going to do well/be well/be happy. You mustn't let the things that happen to you make you live some kind of half-life. You gotta just keep pushing through.

I blame American daytime television. Hello Dr Phil, I'm talking to you. I don't think it's necessarily a bad thing, but do I think that the whole movement towards being confessional has meant that a lot of us are defining ourselves by these personal confessions and truths. We're looking at life through a dysfunctional lens. We're using our issues as a starting point for self-improvement (which is good!), but we're often still carrying them with us like a ball and chain (less good!). The confessions are setting us free, because we're shining a light on them, but somehow they're also what's keeping us from accepting ourselves. (Hello imposter!)

I think it's good to gather up your confessions and issues and examine them for what they are. This can be annoying, because they're often really convenient excuses to pull out when you're feeling challenged or to fall back on when you're facing something new:

→ 'I'm not good at that because of that thing over there that happened when I was fifteen. It was really awful. Plus, I have this back problem.'

→ 'Don't ask me to do that because a person I loved told me I was not good at all of the things any of the time.'

→ 'I can't have a proper relationship because I went to thirty-eight schools and I'm a four-eyes.'

→ 'I can't attend your party because a special person in my life passed away when I was five.'

→ 'I can't take that awesome job. I'm the child of a philanderer. I have freckles.'

Does even one of these sentences sound like you? Probably not, I exaggerated them quite a lot, but you get where I'm going with this.

What are the hurdles you see before you, the things that make you feel incomplete or not okay? Maybe you want to exercise more but you have asthma or some kind of injury? Write that down. Perhaps you can't shake the nasty bullying you suffered in high school at the hands of idiotic-arse-faced-dork people? Write that down. Maybe you think you aren't very lovable/cute-to-look-at/clever? Write that down. Maybe you want to change jobs or travel abroad or move towns, but you know in your heart that you're actually totally useless so just shut up. Sheesh.

Have a think about these old-school things that are defining you. Write them down, look at them, think about them, get help from a trusted confidante or a health professional if some are particularly tricky. Purposefully do the work to acknowledge and deal with the problems you have. Then *politely find time each day to put them aside and excavate the other, ace bits of you that are waiting to be discovered.* Acknowledge, assess, ponder . . . then find practical ways to deal with your old problems and move on.

Things are not always peachy. Further, crappy things happen to good people. Look at and process those crappy things, for sure, but don't let them be a ticket to living a half-life. Don't let things in the past, or fixable things, dictate who you are right now.

Confessions about our true selves can be the framework we build on to become who we are. I'm not saying it's a bad thing to get to grips with the real you. What I am saying is that if that becomes the bigger part of us, we tend to feel less whole and be driven to fill that less-whole-ness. We can get a bit obsessed with proving to ourselves (and perhaps others) that we're enough, despite our confessions. That we're building a more improved model.

Also, every time we come up against an obstacle or challenge, there's a temptation to pull out the excuses and to lay down some extra dysfunctional hurdles. To totally GET IN OUR OWN WAY. Don't do that. Acknowledge, deal with it, move on. Or at least try.

ACTIVITIES

1. Ten-line summary of me (page 51)
2. Your mission statement (page 52)
3. Your life rules (page 53)
4. Your biography (page 53)
5. Taking stock (below)
6. Reverse bucket list (great things you've done!)

TAKING STOCK LIST

Making:	Fixing:
Cooking:	Hoping:
Drinking:	Marvelling at:
Reading:	Needing:
Wanting:	Smelling:
Looking:	Wondering:
Remembering:	Wearing:
Annoying:	Following:
Playing:	Bothering:
Wasting:	Noticing:
Sewing:	Knowing:
Wishing:	Thinking:
Paying:	Nagging:
Enjoying:	Feeling:
Waiting:	Bookmarking:
Liking:	Opening:
Wondering:	Giggling about:
Loving:	Feeling:

Pip's Brownies

200 G DARK COOKING CHOCOLATE

200 G UNSALTED BUTTER

200 G RAW CASTER SUGAR

3 EGGS

½ TSP VANILLA EXTRACT

150 G PLAIN FLOUR

100 G DUTCH COCOA

× Pre-heat the oven to 180°C. Melt the chocolate and butter very gently, in a bowl over a pan of simmering water. (Or you can melt it in the microwave in 30-second bursts, stirring well after each burst.)

× Meanwhile beat the sugar and eggs in a mixer until light and fluffy, then add vanilla. Mix in the melted chocolate/butter mix.

× Now fold in the flour and cocoa. Pour into a very well greased tin – I use a pastry brush to paint melted butter on every millimetre of the tin – twice!

× Bake for about half an hour until the centre is ALMOST cooked – a skewer in the centre should come out a bit chocolaty, but the sides should be pulling away from the tin and the top should be shiny and cracked. YUM!

MAKES 12

CHAPTER FIVE

How to
get ideas

Be less curious about people and more curious about ideas.

MARIE CURIE

Once you've got yourself out of the way, so to speak – or, more accurately, got yourself in the just right place – you can get on with being creative and having nice times. And part of that is having ideas.

I think ideas are easy to come by. Many of us (like me!) are brimming with them very often. Inventions, insights, must-haves, must-makes. Stories to tell, websites to create, things to craft, words to share, books to write, notes to play, moves to try. These sparks are all around.

But it's coming up with ideas at the appropriate time that's quite tricky, don't you think? And making ideas happen? Even trickier. I'm a bit of an ideas junkie. I love ideas, I do. They fill my waking moments, rushing in without warning and quickly fleshing themselves out like one of those toy paper gardens that grow instantly; just add water.

The ideas aren't always good, of course. They're not always practical or logical either. Sometimes they're more about creating a feeling than a thing. They might be about bringing people together, heavy on the good intentions and lighter on the details like where and how (and how much). Or they might be more about documenting or teaching something. It varies quite wildly.

What I like about the prolific spinning of ideas is the way it makes me feel. It's like my brain is open – it feels bigger than it could possibly really be. I like it when my head's full of ideas, sparks, imaginings, what-ifs and wonderings. The more I have ideas, the more ideas I have.

It sounds a little overwhelming, I'm sure, but it's really not. For me, there is no middle ground in this ideas caper – it's an all or nothing thing. You can have it switched on, or you're shut off. Ideas are either free-flowing and bubbling away without limitation or they're not flowing at all. I'll take too many ideas over none any day.

Creativity and ideas need practice, though. They also need attention and acceptance. If you don't use them, if you don't encourage them to flow, they get a bit rusty and it feels like there's some kind of creaky old gate blocking any sparks that might try to escape. You can actually almost HEAR things groaning and scraping as you try to pull inspiration from that neglected part of your brain.

But why would you neglect your ideas-to-be? Why would you let that gate creak? There are a whole bunch of reasons; here are some you might be familiar with.

Creativity and ideas
need practice.

WHY YOU MIGHT GIVE UP ON IDEAS-TO-BE

→ FEAR THAT YOUR IDEA IS STUPID AND YOU'LL LOOK SILLY.

→ FEAR THAT YOU MIGHT ACTUALLY HAVE TO FOLLOW THROUGH ON YOUR IDEA, AND IT SEEMED LIKE HARD WORK.

→ WORRY THAT SOMEONE DID IT ALREADY.

→ BEING UNSURE THAT YOU CAN CARRY OUT THE IDEA — IT'S QUITE HARD.

→ FEELING LIKE NO ONE WILL LOVE THE IDEA AS MUCH AS YOU DO.

→ COULD NOT BE BOTHERED TO DO THE IDEA.

→ FEEL SURE SOMEONE ELSE HAS DONE/COULD DO IT BETTER.

→ DIDN'T REALLY LIKE THE IDEAS THAT WERE HAPPENING AND COULDN'T THINK OF ANY OTHER GOOD ONES.

→ DIDN'T WANT TO COMPROMISE A COMPLICATED IDEA.

→ DIDN'T WANT TO SHARE IDEA WITH OTHER PEOPLE WHO MIGHT CHANGE IT.

→ DIDN'T HAVE ENOUGH MONEY TO MAKE THE IDEA REALITY.

→ THE IDEAS WERE FOR WORK AND NOT FOR YOUR OWN CREATIVITY.

Those are a lot of really understandable, valid reasons. I can totally relate, but you can't just give up. You have to hang in there, take a look at where ideas are going wrong and find out a way to reroute them to fruition. There's nothing worse than a half-baked idea left to float aimlessly around someone's brain. Get it out! Write it down! Use it now or file it neatly away for another time.

You don't know where an idea will take you, or what will pop up as you try to explore or execute it. If you don't even take a chance and try to see it through, you might be cheating yourself out of some interesting/serendipitous/surprising results or experiences. And why on earth would you do that?

Ideas come from
everything.

ALFRED HITCHCOCK

Treat your ideas like rare gems. They're often hard to fathom
when they first arrive, but if you value them and keep track of them,
they'll be useful in some way, some day. They might form into a big,
precious idea. They might get cobbled together with some other
ideas and create something ace. But if you don't let them flow,
if you don't practice having ideas and find ways to document them
or file them for later, you'll be turning your brain into the kind of
place that creaks. It's much more fun to have a brain that flows,
even if it's a little hard to keep a handle on at times.

71

HOW TO SPARK IDEAS:
LOOKING FOR CLUES AND NOTICING THINGS

I really feel like you need to get yourself out and about, exposed to new things, new sites, new places and new people if you want to spark ideas. You are at the ready for inspiration: you just need to make room (and time) to let all of the things in.

In Gretchen Rubin's fabulous *The Happiness Project*, she says:

> Many times, I'd guiltily leave my desk to take a break, and while I was waking around the block, I'd get some useful insight that had eluded me when I was being virtuously diligent.

If you're at home, try to read lots of books, eat lots of different foods, watch great films and documentaries, write letters, flip through magazines, take photographs and leaf through boxes of old things. Don't be tempted to always rest and zone out. Don't be passive. Don't coast along. Take hold of a creative life: get to work at it! Spend some of your free time, every time you have time, searching for clues – looking for the things that spark your interest and make you want to learn/do/create/see more. Be motivated and commit to your interesting life. Follow the clues and don't give up.

If you're not at home, look at the things around you as you go about your day. People you cross paths with might inspire stories, memories or style makeovers. Buildings you see might be worthy of photographing, researching or drawing. Go to the library and see where that leads. Head to a bookshop and look at books you might not normally choose. Attend free events. Take photos, write about what happens, notice problems and ponder solutions. Honour people who've achieved things you admire; truly see the things around you.

Think of it as a kind of frugality of the mind, not wasting

anything. All the things you do and see are brimming with ideas and inspiration, and you might only have a few seconds to scoop those ideas up. Some are more obvious than others: they'll make themselves known and you'll be turning them over and over in your head. Others are more subtle and might be noticeable for their beauty, their shape or their form. Don't waste these gems, consuming and forgetting them as you go about your life. Save them up and note them down for a rainy day.

I don't know what your sparks will look like, because you're quite different to me, but here are how some things I saw hatched some good ideas in my life:

→ A book about Charley Harper I saw on the internet inspired a mid-century fox quilt for a book I wrote.

→ A five-minute TV segment about the Mirabel Foundation and the work they do inspired a charity toy drive, Softies for Mirabel, which I've been running for eight years.

→ A letter sent to me by Tokyo blogger Hello Sandwich inspired a community art installation called 'The Envelope Project'

→ Talking about being a bad Brownie and how much I loved the Girl Guide movement inspired Brown Owls, the worldwide craft gang I started with my friend Kirsty Macafee.

From little things, big things grow. How you grow them is up to you, but if you don't notice the little things in the first place, you're going to be missing out on some great projects, people and realised dreams!

TRUST YOUR HUNCH

Sometimes a great thing grows from a hunch. A hunch about yourself, a hunch about other people, a hunch about what's missing, a hunch about something that just might work.

My friend Hailey Bartholomew was a mum at home with two little girls when she had a hunch she could be a great visual storyteller. She taught herself filmmaking and created an award-winning film on a shoestring. She now travels the world making films and taking photos with her gorgeous family.

One of my favourite people, author Amy Krouse Rosenthal, created a '17 Things I Made' project. Cool! Seventeen things later she had a hunch that the project would be more interesting if a whole bunch of people helped her make an eighteenth thing. Inspired by loveliness, she invited strangers to meet her and her yellow umbrella in a local park at 8pm on 08/08/08 to make Thing Eighteen. Hundreds of excited, curious people showed up on this final making mission. They were as surprised as she was about the turn of events. Everyone was happy.

Singer and all-round fabulous lady Clare Bowditch had a hunch that creative people wanted to know more about connecting with like-minded people, making sense of their world and making money without being frustrated, fraught sellouts. She created Big Hearted Business to support, educate and inspire creatives, and used crowdsourced funding to launch the first Big Hearted Business Conference, enlisting amazing speakers to present live as well as to create weekly Inspiration Bombs for BHB fans. The results of Clare's useful, sustainable hunch are now expanding across Australia. Maybe you have a hunch? A hesitant idea in disguise? Is it something you want to pull out into the light of day? Is it something you want to take a punt on?

TAVI

I heard Tavi Gevinson speak at the Melbourne
Writers Festival. It was super-cool listening to her
talk about her books and how they come to be. She
explained that one thing she might see reminds her
of another seemingly unrelated thing, which reminds
her of a song, which reminds her of a place, which
reminds her of a book, and so it goes. To the outsider,
these things have no relationship to one another,
but to Tavi they are intrinsically linked and their
connected logic is super-clear.

It's a kind of visual/handwritten illustration of
how the internet works. One page links to another,
where a word links to another, an image to another
still, and so it goes on. Great ideas happen when you
expect and notice these common threads. And the
ideas become irresistible when you find ways to note
them down or document them in some way – this
gives them life.

Looking for clues and threads like this is vital.
Finding ways to loosen up your view of the world and
the things you see is really important too: it helps you
carve an easy path to creativity and cleverness. If you
want to hatch fresh sparks, get noticing!

SEEING SIGNS

I'm a sentimental sucker. I don't mind the odd sob and I am completely all about a bit of woo-woo when it comes to making sense of my world.

If I'm op-shopping and stumble across a particular seventies tea mug that's identical to one I sipped my childhood Milo from, I will be convinced that it was laid in my path to encourage me and make me feel loved.

If I'm talking about a particular thing, person, place or feeling and that very thing is discussed glowingly on the evening newsy program, I will KNOW that it's a message for me. It's a secret sign that I'm on the right track and should keep on going.

If I'm discussing a dorky video clip from my youth with someone on Facebook and that VERY song comes on the radio later that day, 'I'm not surprised' (please say that in Jemaine from *Flight of the Conchords'* voice). It means that I belong and am in sync with the universe. It's a sign to let me know.

OF COURSE, I know this is all very woo-woo and possibly nonsensical, but I take my wins where I can get them, and if that means I'm pretending that the world is cheering me on, then that's the way I'm going to roll. You could roll like that too. There's heaps of rolling room.

HOW TO DOCUMENT IDEAS

The thing about ideas is that they can seem super-amazing and then can slip through your fingers, possibly out from your brain via your ears, never to be seen again. I am not sure how such important things can go AWOL without a trace, and even less sure why we don't miss them, but I do know that finding ways to trap and document ideas is vital.

In *The Creative Habit*, Twyla Tharp talks about working on projects starting with a project-labelled filing box purpose-built for the task at hand. She fills the box with research, ideas and inspirations, working as she goes, or sometimes just putting it all away for another time or place. She views these boxes as archives of work done or perhaps work that could be. They seem to serve the purpose of collating and focussing, as well as filing. I think this is also a way to give ideas a firm, boxy base. You can pick the ideas up. They're identified by their label. You can carry them around the room, even. They're tangible and full of promise.

I really love to write things down. I carry notebooks and pens and scribble messy missives in hard-to-read cursive. Sometimes I'm walking and writing at the same time. Usually I'm not wearing my glasses as I scribble, so I have to decypher the notes later with a strong cup of tea. It's quite hard.

I note down all sorts of things. Ideas for craft projects. Things to write in future books. Research I want to do. Blog posts that seem interesting. Things to watch, read or listen to. I know that if I don't get this stuff down, I'll be distracted by other important stuff and the thoughts and things will slip away.

I also use the Notes app in my phone if I want to make a note that will be accessible on my computer, iPhone or iPad. Some thoughts and sparks are in need of amplification. You need to see them often to let them marinate and develop. The beauty of this is that you can keep adding bits and pieces, and before you know it, you've got something on the way to being fully formed. I may have written lots of bits of this book in just this way.

Perhaps you want to download a recording app to your phone and take some time to dictate your thoughts and ideas, so that you can chat away freely and sort the whole lot out at a later time. Or you might use your phone's camera and take photos of the things that spark your creativity, the gems that get you thinking. You can use the photos as prompts for your work or musings; they can form part of a project or just be part of the process. It's up to you.

WHAT IF YOU'RE IN AN IDEAS RUT?

Creative block is a very real problem for sensitive types. It stems from all kinds of things: ill health, exhaustion, too much booze, hard knocks, broken hearts. The problem is usually less about creativity and more about the fragile human spirit. The block is a symptom of a bigger issue. We need to get to the heart of that thing, to apply a salve.

Take tiny steps to mend the bit of you that is bumped up or a bit broken. You don't have to fix it all at once, but making small movements towards repair will create a ripple effect, and bit by bit you'll start to find yourself again.

The thing about these ruts is that you might come out the other side of them with a fresh perspective. You might be a slightly changed person, and your thoughts and ideas might have shifted too. Imagine if this opens up a whole new world of possibility and things to do/ think/make/feel? It may be that, as frustrating as these go-slow times are, passing through them can enrich our days in unexpected ways.

THIRTY-TWO THINGS TO DO
IF YOU NEED TO SPARK IDEAS

go for a walk

watch a documentary

meditate

take a bath

dance about

meet a friend for a nice time

go to a café and sit by yourself. take notes.

read an interesting magazine

bake bread

go to the library and look at reference books

revisit your favourite childhood picture books

look at Pinterest

go to a gallery

make a pompom

visit your local botanic gardens

do some slow cooking and see what percolates

doodle

make a god's eye

lie on the couch and listen to the neighbourhood

look through old photos

attend the theatre

watch old movies

do something you loved to do as a child

walk on the beach or in the bush

spend time with kids. they are full of bright ideas

go to a secondhand market

weave a thing

plant some things

seek out lectures and interesting events

go to book launches and listen to writers talk

go to the museum

make jam

The Best Ever Chicken Soup

This is my super-delicious version of a Sophie Dahl recipe. I've added extra wings and made this a bit speedier. The croutons are 100 per cent Sophie, though.

1 CHICKEN, PLUS ½ KG OF CHICKEN WINGS

1 LEMON

60G BUTTER

SALT AND FRESHLY GROUND PEPPER

A GOOD SLOSH OF OLIVE OIL

1 RED ONION, PEELED AND DICED

1 LEEK, WASHED AND CHOPPED FAIRLY FINELY

2 CLOVES OF GARLIC, CRUSHED

4 CARROTS, PEELED AND SLICED

2 STICKS OF CELERY, CHOPPED ROUGHLY

2 POTATOES, PEELED AND DICED

2 BAY LEAVES

½ TBSP SWEET PAPRIKA

A SLOSH OR TWO OF APPLE CIDER VINEGAR

½ PACKET OF FROZEN PEAS (OR USE FRESH ONES)
OR A COUPLE OF HANDFULS OF SLICED FRESH BEANS

3 LITRES OF WATER

½ LOAF OF SOURDOUGH BREAD

PARSLEY LEAVES, TO SERVE

OPTION: HANDFUL OF KALE

× Pre-heat the oven to 185°C. Wash the chicken, put the lemon and half the butter in its cavity and season it with salt and pepper. Plonk it in an olive-oiled roasting pan and slosh with some more olive oil. Throw the wings in too. Roast in the oven until the chook is lovely and golden and cooked – maybe 50 minutes later or so?

× Set the roasting pan and juices aside: you'll use them later to make delicious chicken croutons. V. important!

× Melt the rest of the butter in a BIG soup pot – it needs to hold all the liquid and veggies and chicken, so no skimping. Add the onion and leek and garlic and cook until softened and fragrant.

× Add the carrots and celery and stir well, then add the potato. Now add the bay leaves, paprika and vinegar. Plonk in the WHOLE cooked chicken, and the chicken wings too. Cover with water and simmer for 1 hour.

× Remove the chicken and the chicken wings: dig around and get those wings out! Let them cool until they're not too hot to handle, then take the meat (and skin if you're decadent) off the chicken and return it to the soup. Add the peas, season with sea salt and pepper and simmer for 10 minutes. Taste to make sure it's salty enough.

× You can add a handful or two of kale at the last minute if you need some leafy greens. While that's happening, make the croutons. They're the best croutons in the universe . . .

× Cut the sourdough bread into cubes. (Crusts on is fine.) Throw them into the pan you roasted the chicken in and cook for 7 or 8 minutes in a hot oven until golden and sticky and delicious. Don't let them burn! Watch them and even turn them over if you are really vigilant.

× Serve your soup with fresh parsley, some croutons and some more freshly ground pepper. Add some chilli if you like it spicy, like me.

81

Nearly Sophie's Soda Bread

This was adapted slightly from Sophie Dahl's recipe in the lovely book *From Season to Season*.

3 CUPS OF BREAD FLOUR (I JUST USE WHITE BAKERS' FLOUR)

2 TSP BICARBONATE OF SODA

1 TSP SALT

1½ CUPS OF BUTTERMILK

OPTIONAL: DRIED MIXED HERBS OR SESAME SEEDS FOR TOPPING

× Pre-heat the oven to 200°C.

× In a mixer (I use a KitchenAid with a dough hook), mix all ingredients until just combined.

× Scoop out the dough with your hands and shape it into a ball. Put it on a greased oven tray and cut a DEEP cross into the top, to help it cook evenly and more springily. Sprinkle with herbs, seeds or sea salt . . . or the thing you like.

× Bake for 40 minutes or until well coloured and 'hollow sounding' when tapped.

Speedy Dinner Rolls

I use a KitchenAid mixer to make these, but you can mix them by hand if you want to!

4 CUPS OF PLAIN WHITE FLOUR

1½ CUPS OF TEPID WATER

1 TBSP DRIED YEAST

2 TBSP SUGAR

½ CUP OF MELTED BUTTER, COOLED

½ TSP SALT

EXTRA BUTTER FOR BRUSHING TOPS

OPTIONAL: SESAME SEEDS, POPPY SEEDS OR GOLDEN SHALLOTS FOR TOPPING

× Mix all the ingredients together, except for the extra butter and toppings. Knead with a dough hook or with your hands (messy!) until the mixture forms a soft dough.

× The finished dough should be smooth and a bit elastic, not shaggy. If it's shaggy, add a sprinkling more flour; if it's a bit dry, add a titch more water.

× Place the dough in a large, greased bowl and cover with plastic wrap. Put it somewhere warmish out of draughts and leave to rise until it's doubled in size. That takes about an hour, usually.

× Punch the dough down and divide into 12 even pieces. Roll these into balls and place them on a greased oven tray – a lamington tray does nicely. Cover loosely with plastic wrap and leave to double in size again.

× Pre-heat the oven to 200 ° C. Brush the rolls with melted butter and sprinkle with sesame seeds, poppy seeds or golden shallots if desired. Bake for 12–15 minutes. They should be golden and delicious-smelling when done!

MAKES 12

CHAPTER SIX

Why creativity?

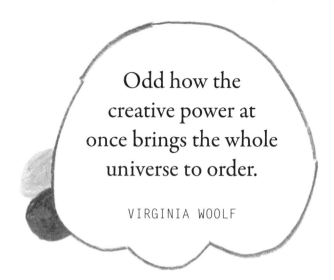

Odd how the creative power at once brings the whole universe to order.

VIRGINIA WOOLF

WELCOME CREATIVITY

Here's the thing. Everyone is creative. Perhaps you know this, because you've grown up in a family that values creative thinking and encourages creative expression. Or perhaps you don't take creativity for granted. Maybe your family valued academic excellence (which, of course, can be extremely creative) above all else and thought that creativity was the domain of bohemian no-hopers. Or perhaps you're somewhere between these two? You think the idea that everyone is creative sounds ace in theory, but when you attempt to be creative, your ideas don't quite match your output. Maybe you're somewhere altogether different, and are still struggling to get in touch with what creativity means to you.

Creativity has become a commodity, a bit like happiness. There are experts and buzzwords and possibly some annoying acronyms. It's sparkly, flashed up on screens in front of conference audiences and also dry, written about in earnest books. All this chatter makes creativity seem difficult and exclusive. But nothing could be further from the truth. Yes, creativity is tricky at times, challenging, even painful for some. But it's also easy and free-flowing and all kinds of fun. Despite what the snake-oil spruikers would have you believe, creativity belongs to us all. You just have to believe it and get on with it, ya know?

Hard work and perseverance are tied into creativity in a big way. You need to practice, stick at it, try stuff and fail. Annoyingly though, the idea of failing can have you second-guessing yourself faster than you can ask 'what's the point?' Creative nerves can fox us into believing our creativity is a bargain-box variety, or derivative or unremarkable. Before we know it, we're sort of paralysed, unable to get on with it, doubting ourselves and terrified of making/creating the thing we want to make/create because we don't know how it will all turn out.

Push on, I say!

HOW TO BE CREATIVE

Start today.

You need to dive into the cool things you want to do. Maybe you started yesterday or last week or last year. That's ace! Go you! Perhaps you're tackling a creative project (or two!), but have wandered off and lost momentum? Or you might not have started at all. Maybe you're teetering nervously on the edge of making/doing stuff?

You need to let it happen. 'But let what happen, WHAT?' you might ask. Maybe you're not even sure what to do/make/craft/cook/sing/play/write in the first place, but you know that's the path you want to explore? Skip to the list at the end of this chapter for some bright ideas.

There may be all kinds of reasons for creative pauses or hesitance, from procrastination to lack of time, to fear, to lack of inclination, to just not having started something. You need to dip your toe in the water. Perhaps you need a little push, something to thrust you into the arms of your creative vision? Here's how to give yourself that push.

GETTING READY TO BE CREATIVE: RITUALS AND PREPARATION

Sometimes what we need to make things work is a really good framework for our day. To put some things in place that make us feel positive about life, we can create some daily habits that comfort, energise, excite, inform, calm or challenge us, depending on our creative 'stature'.

For me, the habits of early morning routines and mid-morning walks are the framework of my day. One (the early mornings, which I talked about in chapter two) prepares me for the challenges of the day ahead, calms my mind and helps me prioritise and document the things I need to do in various ways. The other (the mid-morning walk) keeps me healthy and commits me to creative thinking and learning new things. This is the part of the day when I stock up my ideas and make plans about what to do, when.

Adding in moments for not only gathering ideas and inspiration but also gaining health is super-important to me. It's a great idea to bundle some exercise with your creativity. Yes, you can listen to Missy Elliott on your run if you want, but if you're feeling in a bit of a creative rut, you might find Twyla Tharp's *The Creative Habit* or a bit of *Jane Eyre* on Audible shakes things up in a double-tasking way. Maybe you want to take in some podcasted TEDTalks on your daily walk? Perhaps some *This American Life* would be good on the cross-trainer at the gym? Don't choose between creativity and health, let their powers combine! Healthy creatives are the best kind.

EXPECT INSPIRATION

I've written about this earlier in the book in the 'Look for clues' chapter. Inspiration is all around you: you need to open your eyes and notice it. Seek out the bits that seem special to you.

We need to practise living with inspiration. We need to factor this hunt into our daily routine and make sure we're expecting to see, hear, smell and feel things that wake up our senses. The more we learn to make time for inspiration, the more great stuff we notice and experience.

You might think it's dorky to say that noticing cherry blossoms, kissing couples and luminous sunshiney grass will lead to big things. I'm telling you that training yourself to loosen up and unlock your brain in this way, letting it divert from its usual logical path, will bring all kinds of rewards. Optimism, happiness and beauty are all yours for the taking if you want them. Let your mind wander, your heart be filled and your sense of playfulness and goodness lead your day. Invite inspiration in! Be happier!

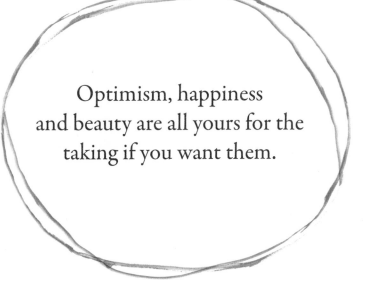

Optimism, happiness and beauty are all yours for the taking if you want them.

IMMERSE YOURSELF IN SOMETHING OR SOMEONE

Sometimes, inspiration leads to a bit of an obsession. I'm not sure how this works for you, but for me, it's like this: I'll hear something, read something or see something a creative person has said or done. I'll feel like they're my soulmate. Then I'll have to read everything possible about them, look at every photo ever taken of them, listen to recordings of them, find out who they were friendly with or influenced by, and transfer some of my obsession to those influencers/pals. It's intense, to say the least. I love the idea of getting under their skin (not literally, ew!), committing to them, finding out what makes them tick and honouring who they were/are.

I think when we have the internet at our fingertips, we tend to shallow-feed a bit. We gather small amounts of information about lots of things. We have great general knowledge about things that aren't that general. I like to dive deeper and put myself in someone else's creative shoes. I love the way it alters my vision of the world, tweaks my point of view. It keeps my mind ticking over and it stops me assuming my way is the highway.

I don't only do this with famous creative people. I do it with skills too. I totally go wild for learning a new skill and dive deep into technique, other crafters who use the skill, fantastic tools that help with the skill and vintage examples of the skill. It's all about committing to knowing more, gathering ideas, sparking even more ideas: making creative magic happen.

Take crochet, for instance. My nanna is an amazing crochet queen. For some reason, though, I never learnt from her when I was growing up. It looked too hard, the movement seemed to hooky and loopy and flicky – like a whole new language spoken with hands and yarn. It wasn't until I was thirty-nine years old that I tackled the tricky job of learning how it was done. I enlisted help from YouTube and my friend Kirsty. I practised. I cried. I threw woolly bits and hooks about the place. I looked at crochet books, read crochet blogs, watched people crochet, fully immersed myself in the world of crochet. I was determined to be more like my Nan. And I totally worked it out in the end. The tears and tough bits were all worth it, and I think I'm now the PERFECT teacher for people like me, who never learnt as kids. And teach I do!

I'm the same with other crafty skills: I got obsessed with/ immersed in embroidery for a couple of years, and subsequently started social embroidery nights. I learnt the complete ins and outs of the Japanese Print Gocco system a few years ago (and then taught them to other people!), printing all kinds of cute things for my friends and family.

Let's talk creative-people-loving: Patti Smith? I have several biographies about her, have downloaded tonnes of podcasts, have read many of her books, listened to her reading things and am quite obsessed with finding photos of her, her family and Robert Mapplethorpe. I've been equally obsessed with other creative sparks at various times: Mirka Mora, Sunday Reed, Little Edie and Big Edie, Julia Child, the Fitzgeralds . . . There are heaps more.

I tend to take each person in one big, deep dose, finding out as much as I can/want to over a period of months, studying their interestingness earnestly. It's inspiring and intoxicating and possibly a bit obsessive, but I don't care. You recognise your people when you see them, don't you think? Why wouldn't you obsess a tad?

I think it's the very best idea to slow down and fill your life with one skill or one creative hero at a time. Get to know it/them inside out and watch it change your creative approach. Feel it change your LIFE! Obsess. Though don't get too weird . . .

MIX UP YOUR INSPIRATION

Don't get STUCK! Shake up your imagination. Shake out your brain. If you're feeling like nothing's moving, like things are not exciting, that you're not inspired . . . do something completely different. If you've been listening to lots of practical information, listen to someone reading classic literature. If you've been watching a heap of documentaries, switch on some BBC drama. If you've been making something intricate, do something simple and freestyle.

Changing things up can recharge creativity and jump-start inspiration and excitement. Don't let creative habits and immersing yourself in your work numb you into a rut. Know when things aren't progressing and serve yourself some fresh new direction.

MAKE TIME TO DO NOTHING

Life is busy, right? We're bombarded with responsibilities, tasks, problems, questions. If we let ourselves, we could be constantly bombarded. And if we're constantly bombarded, we have no quiet time, no time to hang out and muse on things and let random stuff pop into our heads. That kind of quiet time is really important. It helps us unwind and de-stress. It untangles our logical thoughts and allows other hidden stuff to flow freely.

If it's really hard for you to do nothing, you could make a date with yourself to do nothing. Set a timer and let yourself lie on the couch for ten minutes. Download a meditation app and do a mini meditation. Enforce a soak in the bath with no book or phone. Go for a walk without plugging in to anything and see what crops up.

It's been proven that downtime increases creativity. When there's minimal activity in your brain's frontal lobes, you're much more likely to come up with something great.

FIND OUT WHERE YOU FIT IN

A big part of creativity is belonging to a wider creative community.
This may mean you meet up with other clever types in real life –
maybe it's a writing group, or a debating club, or a craft gang? Or
perhaps you commune online via social networking or blogs or the
like. Or you might find your peeps at events or in bookshops or at
really nice cafes. I do not know which is true for you, but I know
how important finding your creative community can be.
You'll feel part of something bigger. You'll have support and
understanding on tap. You'll be able to talk to people who won't
point at you and roll their eyes at your creative leanings. You'll
gather real-life friends and you'll be able to rally your community
to do great stuff, together, for the wider community. That. Is. Great.
If nothing exists in your community to spark your interest, start
something yourself. Put the word out via Facebook or email or
phoning friends. Start small and see what happens: these things
have a way of gaining momentum, and before you know it you
might have created A COOL THING!

Start small and see
what happens.

ACTIVITIES

Make a list of stuff you'd like to make, do or learn about.

HERE ARE A HUNDRED IDEAS MY FRIENDS AND ME CAME UP WITH:

→ KNIT SOCKS!

→ MAKE BUNTING!

→ CREATE STENCILS!

→ GRAFFITI WALLS!

→ CROCHET A BLANKET!

→ THROW POTS (IN A NONVIOLENT WAY)!

→ SEW A QUILT!

→ PLAY THE DRUMS LIKE ANIMAL!

→ PLANT A PERMACULTURE-INSPIRED GARDEN!

→ BREW GINGER BEER!

→ DO MACRAMÉ!

→ PAINT!

→ WRITE A BOOK!

→ LEARN CARPENTRY!

→ DRAW!

→ SING FREELY!

→ SEW A DRESS!

→ MAP THE STARS!

→ BAKE SOURDOUGH BREAD!

→ BEAD A THING!

→ WEAVE ON A PROPER LOOM!

→ PLAY THE BANJO!

→ DO CALLIGRAPHY!

→ MAKE WINE!

→ DRAW CARTOONS!

→ EMBROIDER SOMETHING!

→ PLAY PIANO!

→ BALLET!

→ TURN WOOD!

→ CREATE A TERRARIUM!

→ MAKE LACE!

→ BUILD A BOAT!

→ FINISH A TAPESTRY!

→ BOTTLE SAUCE!

→ MAKE PERFUME!

→ SCREEN-PRINT!

→ FRENCH KNIT!

→ TAKE GREAT PHOTOS!

→ WRITE POETRY!

→ MAKE JAM!

→ FIRE SOMETHING IN A KILN!

→ LEARN MASSAGE!

→ USE A KNITTING MACHINE!

→   WIELD A WELDER!

→   MAKE A TREASURE MAP!

→   PLAY THE UKULELE!

→   SCULPT!

→   TAP DANCE!

→   DO SURFACE DESIGN!

→   MAKE KITES!

→   PLAY GUITAR!

→   ORIGAMI!

→   LEARN A LANGUAGE!

→   MAKE CHEESE!

→   BUILD A SHACK!

→   MAKE SALAMI!

→   GO-GO DANCE!

→   WIRE A LAMP!

→   GIVE A FACIAL!

→   GLASSBLOWING!

→   AMIGURUMI!

→   DJ!

→   PLAY CELLO!

→   SPIN WOOL!

→   DESIGN BAND POSTERS!

→   MAKE A MOSAIC!

→   MAKE SOAP!

→   GIVE TATTOOS!

→   KEEP CHICKENS!

→   VIOLIN!

→   MAKE A FILM!

→   WOODCARVING!

→   CREATE PACKAGING!

→   SURFING!

→   SILVERSMITHING!

→   MILLINERY!

→   DESIGN COSTUMES!

→   IKEBANA!

→   TEA CEREMONY!

→   PLAY THE HARP!

→   SHEAR SHEEP!

→   MAKE TOYS!

→   BOOKMAKING!

→   MASTER PHOTOSHOP!

→   CAKE-DECORATING!

→   HAIR-BRAIDING!

→   STAMP-CARVING!

→   FABRIC-DYEING!

→   MAKE PASTE-UPS!

→   MAKE-UP ARTISTRY!

→   CUT HAIR!

→   METALWORK!

→   PRODUCT DESIGN!

→   MAKE STICKERS!

→   MAKE A ZINE!

→   FLOWER ARRANGING!

→   CREATE WINDOW DISPLAYS!

→   MAKE LINGERIE!

→   ILLUSTRATE A
    KID'S BOOK!

MAKE A LIST OF INSPIRING FAVES

MY PALS AND I MADE THIS LIST OF A HUNDRED-PLUS GREAT PEOPLE. FOLLOW THEIR LEAD, LEARN STUFF FROM THEM, GET EXCITED AND GO MAKE SOMETHING!

Corita Kent	Janis Joplin
Patti Smith	Audrey Tautou
Andy Warhol	Frida Kahlo
Hunter S Thompson	David Attenborough
William Morris	Twyla Tharp
Evelyn Waugh	Mirka Mora
Wassily Kandinsky	Audrey Hepburn
Robin Boyd	Jocasta Innes
Maggie Smith	Gerald Durrell
Camille Claudel	Maggie Beer
Yoko Ono	Margaret Kilgallen
Henri Matisse	Vali Myers
John Lennon	Maya Angelou
Björk	Freddie Mercury
Meryl Streep	Mother Teresa
JD Salinger	Clare Bowditch
David Sedaris	Clarice Cliff
Jenny Kee	Margaret Atwood
Sunday Reed	Joan Didion
Brett Whiteley	Gretchen Rubin
Claude Monet	Carrie Brownstein
The Fitzgeralds	Miranda July
Regina Spektor	Alice Waters
Florence Broadhurst	Pablo Picasso
Judi Dench	Vivienne Westwood
Rosalie Gascoigne	Tavi Gevinson
Charlotte Brontë	Sophie Dahl
Cyndi Lauper	Prue Acton
Tim Winton	Diane von Fürstenberg

Iris Apfel
Stephen Fry
Charles and Ray Eames
Bill Cunningham
Julia Cameron
Tim Buckley
Stevie Nicks
Frank Lloyd Wright
Annie Leibovitz
Aubrey Beardsley
John Irving
Jules Verne
Richard Scarry
Mary Blair
Maurice Sendak
Steve Jobs
Louise Bourgeois
Salvador Dalí
Kate Bush
Diane Arbus
David Bowie
Guy Bourdin
John Marsden
Agatha Christie
Julia Child
Joy Hester
Nathalie Lété
Sylvia Plath
Dorothy Parker

Grace Coddington
Oscar Wilde
Shaun Tan
Louisa May Alcott
Dodie Smith
Augusten Burroughs
Helen Garner
Jonathan Safran Foer
Amy Krouse Rosenthal
Anne Lamott
Coco Chanel
Tracey Emin

Toasty Things

TOAST WITH PEA PESTO

This pea and goat's cheese pesto keeps nicely in a jar in the fridge. You can make a whole platter of toastie bits and serve them to your friends and family, if you fancy. You might like to try the pesto on pasta too!

1 PUNNET OF CHERRY TOMATOES
(OR OTHER SMALL TOMATO VARIETY)

¼ CUP OF GOOD-QUALITY EXTRA
VIRGIN OLIVE OIL

500G FROZEN PEAS, COOKED

100G GOAT'S CHEESE,
PLUS A LITTLE EXTRA

GOOD SLOSH OF GOOD-QUALITY
BALSAMIC VINEGAR

HANDFUL OF FRESH HERBS
(I USE THYME, BASIL AND PARSLEY
FROM MY GARDEN)

SEA SALT AND FRESHLY GROUND
BLACK PEPPER

NICE BREAD FOR TOASTING

× Pre-heat the oven to 200 °C. Toss the tomatoes in the olive oil, sprinkle with half the herbs and roast in the oven for about 15 minutes, until softened and colouring up a bit.

× Meanwhile, make the pesto. In a food processor, blitz the cooked peas and goat's cheese (with a few spoonfuls of the oil it comes in or a good slosh of extra virgin olive oil), plus the vinegar, herbs and salt and pepper, until it becomes a rustic paste.

× Make some toast. Spread the pesto on the toast and plonk the tomatoes on top. Add a little extra goats cheese, salt and pepper, and scoff the lot! YUM!

SERVES 4

TOAST WITH CHEESE SPREAD

This is my version of a totally weird family recipe.
I grew up with it, as did those who went before me.
If you like spicy, piquant, cheesy, melty toast, then
this is for you. Think Welsh rarebit gone wonk.

200G GRATED MOZZARELLA CHEESE

200G GRATED EXTRA TASTY CHEESE

200G GRATED CHEDDAR CHEESE

200ML BOTTLED TOMATO SAUCE
OR KETCHUP

100ML BARBECUE SAUCE

30G CURRY POWDER

½ TBSP MUSTARD POWDER

½ TSP CAYENNE PEPPER

½ TSP SWEET PAPRIKA

A GOOD DOSE OF SALT
AND WHITE PEPPER

NICE BREAD FOR TOASTING

×   Mix all ingredients except bread together. Heat the griller.
×   Toast one side of your bread under the griller, then remove toast.
     Spoon and spread the cheesy mix onto the untoasted side.
×   Grill until the cheese bubbles and toast is golden.
×   Toast toppings
×   I like special things on toast. It's a weakness of mine. Here's two ways
     to 'tartine' like me: one is tomatoey and one is olivey. I think it's only
     fair that you try both – on toast!

MAKES ENOUGH FOR AROUND 20 SLICES OF TOAST

CHAPTER SEVEN

Do new stuff

FEEL THE FEAR AND BE A BEGINNER

I am in love with the new. New recipes. New crafty skills. New concepts. New shoes. I love the simplicity and nostalgia of old favourites, but I am motivated and thrilled by the prospect of new.

When I read that quote on Pinterest that says 'Feel the fear and do it anyway', I always think they're talking about people jumping out of planes or swimming with sharks. This makes me want to back out of the room, creating a diversion as I get as far away from the scary thing as possible. But they could just as well be talking about people who are considering less-extreme-sportzy things:

→ Feel the fear and learn the banjo anyway!

→ Feel the fear and learn Spanish anyway!

→ Feel the fear and try pottery anyway!

→ Feel the fear and talk to that girl on the bus anyway!

→ Feel the fear and rollerskate anyway!

→ Feel the fear and watch every season of *Six Feet Under* anyway!

Nobody said the fear had to be a totally petrifying, life-endangering fear. Perhaps the fear is a bit smaller and more achievable, although still quite daunting.

I think those mini-fears are the sort we need to try. Sometimes you have to take a chance and see what happens, find out whether the fear-y thing is really for you. What if the feeling of hesitance is actually some kind of natural aptitude that's got its wires crossed? How will you know unless you let yourself be a beginner and find out more?

WHY DO NEW STUFF?

Why do new stuff? Because tackling new tasks, habits, places, people and ideas will make you feel challenged and alive. And feeling alive can make you feel really happy. Happy because you feel energised by the change of pace and your risky 'tude. (Let's face it, you're a daredevil!) Happy because you're learning new things about yourself as you newbie along the way. Happy because you've taken a punt and trusted yourself to cope with whatever you're dealt. Happy because you might be trusting other people to help you with something or to teach you a skill. Happy because your usual routine has shifted, and that makes other things shift, too. Happy because you meet new people, see new things, go new places. Happy because you're adapting. Happy because it all feels different and, well, new! Happy because you're alive.

At its worst, new stuff makes you feel a bit chuffed with yourself for stepping up, even if things don't turn out the way you imagined. At its best, new stuff makes you feel satisfied because something great happened along the way: you learnt something new, you were good at something you thought you'd be crap at, you met someone who said something interesting, you saw something that took your breath away, you read something poignant or memorable, you felt excited or competent or fascinated or impressed.

Yes, creative habits and rituals are an awesome framework for creativity and happiness. But sometimes, they become so routine that ideas dry up and monotony sets in. That's when we need the new.

New stuff diverts us from our usual, predictable path. It springs up in front of us, lighting our way with fresh sparks and promise. It reminds us to have fun times, that we're interesting and interested in life. New stuff picks us up, shakes us about and puts us down in different surrounds. It gives us a chance to see what we're capable of and connects us to new passions and people we need to know about. New stuff gives us fresh insight into who we are and where we might go. New stuff keeps us moving.

Psychologist Dr Simone Ritter has researched this extensively. She's found that altering even the simplest routines (like how you make a sandwich, for instance) can cause biological changes in your brain, which can result in new ideas. When you change stuff up or approach something unfamiliar, your brain's usual neural pathways are diverted and new connections between brain cells are created.

Seeking out new experiences or completely altering the way you usually do things is a DIY way to foster these new connections and lead to improved creativity and general feelings of awesomeness. So: walk a different way to work, go to a new lunch place, wear runners instead of boots, read a magazine you'd never normally buy, shift your morning work-out to the evening, say hello to people you don't know, go to bed early instead of late. Mix up your life and see what new connections materialise in your grey matter. Science wants you to.

Out of your vulnerabilities
will come your strength.

SIGMUND FREUD

WHAT'S STOPPING YOU FROM DOING NEW STUFF?

Gosh. Did you get a knot in your stomach when you thought of all the new things you could be doing? I can relate. If you're anything like me, fear is looming over that list all cloaked and dark. *shudder* New, scary things can transport the most grown-up person back to pre-school days. The urge to back away can be pretty overwhelming. I'm doing just fine on this path, thanks. I've got things in place, it's all super-safe, I'm tucked in, I'm buttoned up, I'm good. Thanks, but no thanks. Shut the door when you leave. Nothing to see. I'm just going to get under this blanket now. Goodbye.

All kinds of things can keep you on the reliable road to regular routine. Avoiding new things/people/places because life seems perfectly fine already is totally understandable. I like routine too. It helps with my creative habit and makes me feel cosy and secure. But it's really important to make an effort, at least some of the time, to reach for something more. Remember the science?!

Yes, it's super-easy to stop taking risks, to assume we know better, to decide we've got life covered. But it's also a little bit pessimistic and a lot Negative Nancy. Instead of getting excited about the good things that could happen when we take on the new, we get stuck in hypothetical problems that might be looming. We say, 'I've got enough going on' as we scramble under that security blanket, just in case things don't turn out right. We assume we've got it all together, that the equilibrium is sorted, and we forget that life's meant to be a bit of an adventure. It's not meant to be perfectly balanced. Mistakes are meant to be made, but progress is there for the taking, too.

Things might veer from the comforting, usual path when we try something new, and that seems too big a gamble to take. What if things don't go well?!

Fear of doing things wrong, doing things clumsily, looking silly, being criticised, looking amateurish, saying the wrong thing, being a beginner, not understanding, being ignored, being hurt, being last, being alone. These are the kind of things that stop us in our tracks and make us seek a blanket fort. However, as good as blanket forts are, they're not the best solution in the quest for the new – unless your new thing is 'Blanket-Fort-Making Class'. (Then you should jump right in.)

Applied poorly, habit and routine can stop us from learning and finding fun. Fear of change can rob us of amazing experiences and people or skills we might REALLY need in our lives. Bracing ourselves for the worst can rob us of happy moments and joyful, playful times. Hesitation and hibernation can conceal new talents waiting for us in the wings.

Why would you do that to yourself? Expect the best and take a punt on the new. Don't let you hold you back. Get sciencey on your brain.

A single day is enough
to make us a little larger or,
another time, a little
smaller.

PAUL KLEE

HOW TO DO NEW STUFF: CHANGE ONE SMALL THING AND EVERYTHING WILL CHANGE

Sometimes it's hard to know where to start when you want to shake things up. It really doesn't have to be a huge step into the unknown, though. Start small. Shift things by doing one thing, changing one thing or learning one thing and see what the ripple effect is. There's a good chance you'll become addicted to the new, that you'll discover that you're completely great at changing things up and trying fresh stuff. You might even realise that your old routine wasn't really as comforting as you thought. Maybe it was actually NUMBING! Gazooks! Perhaps you were a teensy bit asleep all this time?! Here are a few ways to wake yourself up.

HABIT-CHANGING PROJECTS

Adopt a new habit. It might be a change in diet, switching to healthier foods, shirking sugar, going vegetarian. It could be a new fitness regime: yoga when you get up, lunchtime walks around the park, go-go dancing class one night a week. Maybe it's giving up alcohol?

ROUTINE-CHANGING

Maybe you're in such a fug that you're reading this from Day Three of your blanket-fort residence? You have to mix things up. Change the time you get out of bed in the morning. Try leaving for work half an hour earlier so you can have a long, quiet coffee at a nice café. Take a short lunch break and leave work early so you can do something fun. Play with time and shift things around so you can schedule in something new in your day. Make sure it's something new for you, though. Extra time for doing the laundry is not the kind of thing I'm talking about at all (unless you really, really love doing the laundry: then you're good to go!).

7 OR 52 OR 365 PROJECTS

These daily or weekly creative or life challenges are the perfect way
to tweak a snoozy routine and shake things merrily up! You can set
your own 365-day or 52-week or 7-day challenge: maybe it's cooking
every recipe from a favourite cookbook. Perhaps it's writing in a
journal every day. Cataloguing every Neil Diamond song.
It could be a random act of kindness every day. What would you
like to do every day? Take a daily photo? Do a drawing? Write a
poem or a song? Eat a biscuit? Okay. Maybe it's not about biscuits,
but it might be for someone. Put your thinking cap on and
challenge yourself to a year of new.

You can find lots of these kinds of challenges online if you're
a blog-reader like me. They're meant to be fun, creative boosts, so
don't beat yourself up if you miss a day or week here and there.
Just take part and see what happens.

GET SOCIAL

Meeting new people is a joy. I know that shyness can put a damper
on making new friends, but I think once you realise that most
people feel a bit dorky when they first meet, things get a lot easier.
Those first attempts at finding common ground can be fumbly and
awkward. Sometimes there's too much to say, and sometimes not
enough. But riding out the weird early seconds/minutes/hours
of a prospective new friendship is really worth the effort.

One thing I've learnt from writing a blog and sharing bits of my
life is that humans are similar in lots of ways. Feeling dorky is pretty
universal. We tend to cover up our dorkiness with humour, or by
being mousy-quiet, or even by pretending to be a different version
of ourselves. But if you try and relax and assume the best of yourself,
things can fall into place MUCH faster.

As great as it is to be connected to people online, it's really important to take that extra step and make real-life connections too. It's a teensy bit fearful to keep yourself cloistered away and spend time with your loyal few. Extend yourself a wee bit more often and look for people you might like. Give people a chance to buddy up with you or work on projects with you or be in your mini-gang. Don't be fearful of new friendships. Invite them in and see what they bring. Maybe they'll bring cake. You never know!

MAKE A DECLARATION

Sometimes the best thing you can do when you're stuck in a bit of a calm, possibly boring routine is to come up with a great idea and *tell people that you're going to do it*! Maybe it's a charity drive or a half marathon or a year without chocolate or a house move or a new course of study. Take some quiet time to hatch ideas and develop a goal or project you're really excited by – then set it free and tell people what you're going to do.

Declarations start conversations, not only with other people, as you excitedly/nervously explain what you have in mind, but also with yourself, as you battle self-doubt and celebrate first steps towards your new goal.

Making a declaration helps you be more accountable and allows you to gather some cheerleaders along the way. It's also super-brave, committed and has the power to inspire other people to try doing cool stuff, too. Publicly announcing your goal gives you a head start on achieving your once-secret dream. It's a vote of confidence in your own direction as you tackle something new.

GO OUTSIDE

I am extremely guilty of staying in. I work from home and I manage my workflow pretty precisely, piling on JUST as much as I can handle (possibly a bit more, even!). I used to catch myself staying

in for three DAYS STRAIGHT working on a variety of great
projects. Week after week I'd do this, coming up for air on Day Four
and busting out.

YES, I was enjoying the things I was doing. But NO, I was
not getting enough fresh, outdoorsy air into my lungs. This was
not good. Staying in made me very still and tired, and then I found
it hard to keep up. And then I felt stressed. And then I felt sad.
Possibly I sobbed. It was not a good situation.

Then I had a desperate, bright idea. I should run away! I should
avoid the things I wasn't keeping up with. I decided to go for a walk.
What happened next was this: I walked down my street (in my ugly
trainers) and around the park. I breathed the fresh air and I looked
at trees; I saw the sparkle on their leaves. I saw the emerald glint of
a duck's under-feathers. I saw the ripply pattern the wind swirled
across the pond. I felt less tired. I felt more alive. I felt sparkly, ducky
and ripply. I went back home and got all my things done and still
had time for a cup of tea and hot bath with a book – even though
I ran away. Whodathunkit?!

Take the time to get out in the fresh air, amongst nature,
trees and things. Breathe in the day; let the light touch you; let the
sunshine warm you. Do this every day. It will energise you. It will
give you more time. It will make YOU new. Start today.

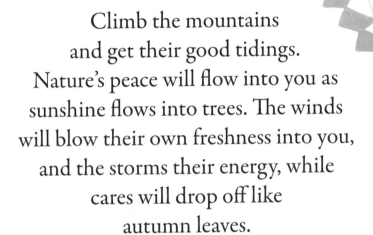

Climb the mountains
and get their good tidings.
Nature's peace will flow into you as
sunshine flows into trees. The winds
will blow their own freshness into you,
and the storms their energy, while
cares will drop off like
autumn leaves.

JOHN MUIR (NATURALIST),
OUR NATIONAL PARKS

7 OR 52 OR 365 PROJECT IDEAS

→ A WEEK OF VEGETARIANISM

→ A WEEK OF NO BOOZE

→ A WEEK OF CLASSIC MOVIES

→ A WEEK OF NO TV

→ A WEEK OF FRESH FLOWERS

→ A WEEK OF TALKING
TO STRANGERS*

→ A WEEK OF CHILDHOOD
STORYBOOKS

→ A WEEK OF EXERCISING
NIGHTLY

→ A WEEK OF DRAWING

→ A WEEK OF READING POETRY

* Not weirdos.

→ 365 PHOTOS OF MY LIFE

→ 365 JOURNAL ENTRIES

→ 365 HEALTHY DAYS

→ 365 DAYS OF CRAFT

→ 365 POEMS

→ 365 BLOG POSTS

→ 365 ARTICLES READ

→ 365 LOAVES OF BREAD

→ 365 JOKES

→ 365 HUGS

→ 52 LISTS

→ 52 FAMILY PHOTOS

→ 52 CAKES

→ 52 WALKS

→ 52 MAGAZINES

→ 52 SONGS WRITTEN

→ 52 LETTERS TO MYSELF

→ 52 DINNER DATES

→ 52 PET PORTRAITS

→ 52 OUTFITS (OR HAIRDOS!)

Our Family's Favourite Party (Chocolate) Cake

This recipe is Elizabeth David's, but I came
across it via Stephanie's restaurant, when it used
to be their house chocolate cake. My mother-in-law
at the time was Stephanie's partner, and she used
to bring us home bits of this cake on Sundays,
as the restaurant was closed the next day.
I love cooking this, but I have to take
extra care not to burn the chocolate!

125G GOOD COOKING CHOCOLATE, CHOPPED

1 TBSP BRANDY

1 TBSP BLACK COFFEE

100G UNSALTED BUTTER

100G CASTER SUGAR

100G GROUND ALMONDS

3 EGGS, SEPARATED

ICING SUGAR TO DUST

- × Pre-heat the oven to 160°C. Butter and line an 18 cm baking tin – springform is best.
- × Combine the chocolate, brandy and coffee in a bowl over a pan of simmering water. When melted, stir and add the butter and sugar. Mix very well. Add the ground almonds and mix well.
- × Lightly beat the egg yolks, take the bowl off the heat, and then mix in.
- × Beat the egg whites with a mixer until stiff. Fold one tablespoon of the whites into the chocolate mix to loosen it up, then gently fold in the remaining whites. Goop it into the tin and bake for 40 minutes or so. It will be crusty on the top, but fudgy in the middle. Cool completely and serve dusted with icing sugar.
- × I often double this recipe and use a larger springform tin!

CHAPTER EIGHT

Hang with your friends

I love my friends. They are the best. They make me want to be a better person as I bathe in the delicious friendly light they emit. Le sigh. Do you feel like that about your friends too?

Sometimes I get a bit busy with work and family and I don't see much of my friends. I'm still okay, but I lose a bit of my sparkle. It's like my friends are a giant bottle of glitter, and when I go near them, little bits of sparkle get all over me – even when I don't open the bottle. That stuff finds a way. That's what happens with glitter, right?

Once, when I went on a stressful work trip, I came home after a long few days feeling all at sea. Like I was swishing about in a little boat, a little bit Pippy Hemingway, a little bit *Life of Pip*, a little bit Pip-eye. Not good. I needed friendly first aid. So I called my pals straight away to say, 'Come over for dinner, PLEASE.' 'Okay!' they said. I pushed my worky exhaustedness away, cooked a few nice things, and before I knew it there were ace people in my lounge room with their shoes off and their smiles on. I'm still trying to get the glitter out of my rug. You need some glitter in your life too. You know it's true.

Don't wait for the right time or the right place. The right people can always be wrangled into a schedule with a bit of clever shoehorning. And not only do you get to hug them and find out what's going on with them, you get to dab a bit of their glittery aceness behind your ears too.

WHY FRIENDS ARE IMPORTANT

We are social creatures. As great as quiet times and being introverted can be, we all need some like-minded people in our life to give us a squeeze, some canny advice and to chortle naughtily with too. We need to get out, to find our people and to frolic about with them in a joyful, playful, fun kind of way. Or sometimes we don't. Sometimes we need to sit about at home with our friends, lamenting society or relationships or the evening news together. The point is, everyone needs someone. Even Catweazle, the seventies hermit of my childhood nightmares, had friends.

Friends are just what you need to snap yourself out of a nasty bout of overzealous self-reflection. Friends will remind you that while watching the box set of *Breaking Bad* for an entire weekend is ace, there's more to life than Heisenberg and fried chicken. Friends are a perfect dose of reality, showing you where you fit in, who you belong to and why life is great.

We spend a lot of time thinking about how to better ourselves, and a big part of that is actually fronting up and interacting with other humans. It's really easy to stay in, talk via social media, or text or email our pals. But what we really need to do is get out with them, invite them over, face-to-face it IRL. And possibly get a bit stupid with them.

Sadly, friends have become another to-do. Seeing friends might even feature further down your to-do list than work, home stuff or health. But friendship is SUPER-important. It feeds us in ways that are hard to measure. Friendship shows us where we fit in, what's good about us, what we like to do and how we react. It gives us a chance to be ourselves with other nice humans in a safe and friendly way: we get to be understood, listened to, valued, liked and cared about by people we admire and chose.

Friendship shows us how great other people can be, how

119

lucky we are to be in their orbit and how, when it comes down to it, relationships are king. Friends are collaborators, confidantes, champions and coaches. They're the ones that laugh indulgently at your naff jokes, dance with you when you need some fun times, buy you cute treats and front up at your place with wine and/or episodes of *Orange Is the New Black*.

Friends can copilot you through tricky times, suggest a fresh point of view, give you a reassuring squeeze or sometimes just hang out and say nothing at all. The point is, they're about the place – they're on call. They've saved you a seat and they want to know what's going on in your world. They miss you when you're gone.

The friendly feeling of belonging, being liked and listened to can carry us buoyantly through our days and help us find our fit. If we're too busy doing other pressing things, we might underestimate the importance of friendship to our happiness. You really shouldn't do that. A tiny dose of friendship is the perfect pick-me-up.

A friend is a gift
you give yourself.

ROBERT LOUIS
STEVENSON

WHERE TO FIND FRIENDS

Most people already have a group of friends. They might be work pals, or childhood friends from the old neighbourhood. They could be people we met at the gym or a class, or friends of friends who have become our friends too (which is friendly!).

Perhaps the friends you've got are great, but you want to bolster yourself with a couple more? This is a totally bright idea! The best way to make new friends is to do new things. Trying new things is one of the keys to a great life. Combine new things with new friends and you're totally off the Richter scale in the Nice Times department. I think you need to look for new friends as soon as possible.

New friends may be waiting for you at that new café around the corner. They might be about to attend that wood-fired bread-making course you always wanted to do. They could be knitting along at the local craft group that meets in the library. Are they doing push-ups in the early-morning boot camp? Are they lining up for tacos at that new taquería place? Is that them sitting excitedly waiting for the lecture to begin? Are they volunteering alongside you at the local public radio station?

Obviously, you are surrounded by friends. You just haven't met them all yet. Start meeting them. It's up to you!

APPRECIATING FRIENDS

Take some time to think about the friends you have. Write down their names. Think about the things they do for you, what they mean to you, why you like them, what you have in common. Now tell them some of the things you came up with. Let them know their value in your life, and do it often. Send messages, write postcards, make phone calls and make time to get together in real life to do good stuff too.

SCHEDULING FRIENDSHIP TIME

Are you a busy person? I am too. I tell myself that this is why
I sometimes go a couple of weeks without seeing my friends.
Then, when I do check in with a member (or more) of my gang,
I realise how empty life was without them, how excited they get me
about life and what a productive, positive effect they have on me.
How can you be too busy for that?

If you tend to immerse yourself in work, busy family life or
other obligations, you might feel there's no time for friendly catch-
ups. I think it's really super-important to add friends to your to-do
list if you're the busy kind. I know it seems a bit un-friendly to treat
friends as a scheduled task, but sometimes it helps you keep on track,
especially if the alternative is not seeing them at all.

Putting friends last is a little bit like putting yourself last.
It's counterproductive. Friends are full of clever observations, excellent
advice and hilarious anecdotes (if you're lucky like me!). These are
the very things that give life meaning. If you're saying no to friends
quite often, then you're saying no to clever, excellent and hilarious.
WHAT are you like? Don't do that!

Schedule friends, blocking out mini-meetings for quick squeeze
and chuckles. If you are super-clever, you can schedule a whole
bunch of friends for an early mid-week dinner, gathering goodness
and smooches, yet still being home with plenty of time for some
catch-up telly, a biscuit and a nice cup of tea. Get amongst it.

FAMILY MATTERS

Your history and where you came from matters too. There really is nothing like family: they're an intrinsic part of who you are. They share your story. They've seen you grow and have followed all your highs and lows. There's a kind of KNOWING YOU that family has that no one else can get close to.

It's partly a time thing – the millions of hours you've had together, the changes you've been through, the experiences you've shared. Part of it is hereditary too, I think: you can be just like another person in your family in ways that can't be put down to nurture or mimicry. Think of twins who are separated at birth only to be reunited and share all kinds of similarities!

How about this: James Lewis and James Springer were separated just weeks after birth. As adults they were reunited:

> Both of the 'Jim twins' had married and divorced women named Linda. Both had second marriages with women named Betty. Both had police training and worked part-time with law enforcement agencies. Both had childhood pets named Toy. They had identical drinking and smoking patterns, and both chewed their fingernails to the nub. Their first-born sons were named James Alan Lewis and James Allan Springer.[*]

You can't tell me that's coincidental. You just can't.

There are lots of crazy, amazing cases like this that prove our genetic similarities, but most of us don't need such hard evidence: we know we're a lot like some people in our family. A lot of our good bits have familial links. Perhaps we have the energy and constitution of a favourite aunt, or we share a love of mushy novels with a loved-up

[*] Peter Miller, 'Twins', *National Geographic*, January 2012.

grandma. Perhaps we share sentences with a sister. These are the people we need to spend time with. They provide instant acceptance, understanding and a sense of history and connection that can't be beaten. Find these people in your family and make the most of your true family connections (even if it takes a bit of extra effort!).

. . . there is no happiness
like that of being loved
by your fellow-creatures, and
feeling that your presence is an
addition to their comfort.

CHARLOTTE BRONTË,
JANE EYRE

FAMILY PROBLEMS

Families can be really great. Yep. But they can also be super-hard work. You're kind of dealt a hand with families, and you have to work it out. Sometimes it's really hard to hang out with your family; other times it's joy-filled and noisy and great. I'm not sure how it is for you, but I do know that every family has good things about it and good people in it. I also know that families are your roots. They provide a real insight into why you are and who you are. Working out where you fit into your family, what your family DNA is all about and how to deal with it is an important part of getting to know yourself.

I think we do a lot of digging into the problems that families can cause. There are difficult issues in every family, along with drinkers, spenders, villains and old cows. They might be a long way down the line, or they might be your immediate family. Whichever it is, they're a part of you. (Maybe a tiny particle-sized part, maybe something bigger.)

Looking at the problems you have with family, getting to the heart of them and dealing with conflict is a great way to ensure or preserve your own happiness. Sometimes problems can't be worked out in the short term, but you can find ways to deal with them and cope as efficiently as possible. You don't need to define yourself by or focus unhealthily on family conflicts or issues. Take the time to look at the problems you might be having objectively and work out how you can bundle them up into an easier-to-deal-with package. Letting family problems seep into all the corners of your life and define who you are is a really bad idea. Be a grown-up and find ways to acknowledge the problems, deal with them as respectfully and practically as you need to, and then get on with your life.

FAMILY STRATEGIES

What do you do if you have to spend time with family you're not keen on? Like, maybe it's Christmas time or Nanna's birthday, or you're all rubbing shoulders at some event or other.

Firstly, don't fall down the rabbit hole. Don't succumb to the usual patterns of conflict and quiet hysteria that have been set in stone for years. Step away from that stuff: start afresh. It might seem like a good idea to drink four glasses of champagne and start bleating 'He's picking on me' while pointing wildly at Great-uncle Merv, but just don't. Here's what to do:

→ Say hello to the annoying people and then buzz happily away to the good 'uns.

→ Don't freak out and drink too much to calm your nerves or your desire to get stabby.

→ Don't overstay your welcome. It's much nicer to stay for a short time and be pleasant than to endure the long haul and leave ready to tear your hair out.

→ Take a buffer person. Okay, this is kind of cheating, but if you take a non-family member to family events, people tend to behave much more nicely.

→ Clean. Yep, this is cheating too, but sometimes tidying your mind with tidy tasks is the only thing that will stop you poking Aunt Ethel with her own hatpin.

IT'S OKAY FOR IT NOT TO BE OKAY

You know what? Sometimes people are just not compatible. Sometimes they have combative relationships (ugh!). They have their eccentricities, insecurities and tired old habits. Sometimes family sparring is a kind of sport (not my kind of sport, mind you); sometimes it's an unchallenged pattern of bad behaviour. It can be rooted in something serious, but often it's not. It's super-awesome to think we can improve the trickier relationships we have with family members. But sometimes we just can't.

In this case, you might just need to say, 'It is what it is.' You may not be able to make it what you want it to be. That doesn't mean it can't be okay, but you might need to shift your expectations dramatically – not place quite so much importance on how it should be – and just accept how it is.

Make the most of the family members who are easy to get along with and deal with the tougher cookies from afar or in short doses. Think of their behaviour from a kind of scientific, David Attenborough point of view, rather than taking it personally. Accept what you have and try not to long for what you think you should have.

Be grateful for anyone who's not completely nuts, family-wise.

FRIENDS ARE THE FAMILY YOU CHOOSE

Maybe, despite my chatter about finding the people in your family who you feel most connected to, and about dealing with family problems, you might still have issues with your peeps that seem insurmountable. Then you need to make your own family: just DIY. Friends are the family you choose, or so they say; you just need to get choosing.

You may already have found your chosen family. Or you might need to put it at the top of your to-dos. Just know that everybody needs a gang of good people to get close to. Please find yours.

Just because you're far from your own family in varying ways, you don't have to be alone. You are not Tom Hanks on a desert island with a fetching beard and a bunch of coconuts. You are an interesting, loveable, modern person who needs a great bunch of interesting, loveable, modern people to share your life with. DIY family style.

If you cannot get rid of the
family skeleton, you may as
well make it dance.

GEORGE BERNARD SHAW,
IMMATURITY

ACTIVITY

ACE WAYS TO HANG WITH YOUR PALS:

→ DINNER DIAL-IN

→ MARKET FORAGING

→ AFTERNOON OF DIP-MAKING AND COCKTAIL-SHAKING

→ NAIL PARTY

→ DOG-WALKING

→ BACKYARD BEER-SIPPING

→ WINDOWS-DOWN DAYTRIP

→ BOOKSHOP SNEAK-AROUND

→ PILLOW-TOTING PICNIC

→ BAND-OGLING

→ ESTHER WILLIAMS TRIBUTE SWIMMING POOL VISIT

→ GEEKY STARGAZING DATE

→ JAFFLE-SAMPLING BRUNCH

→ OP-SHOP TRAWL

→ *FLASHDANCE*-STYLE WORK-OUT

→ PATIO PIMMS

→ LIBRARY WANDERING

→ AVOCADO TOAST APPOINTMENT

→ JAM-MAKING SESSION

→ HAND-HOLDING TATTOO-GETTING GANG

→ RECORD NIGHT

→ JAFFLE-OFF!

→ MUSEUM SAFARI

→ QUICK SQUEEZE IN THE STREET

→ NINETIES MOVIE FESTIVAL

→ POT LUCK SUPPER

→ OVER-THE-FENCE-FLOWER-STEALING WALKATHON

→ CRAFTERNOON

→ CURRY CLUB

→ HAIRDRESSER DOUBLE-BOOKING

→ BEACHY FISH AND CHIP SCOFF

→ UNDER-TREE BANANA LOUNGE CHAT

→ PICTURE-HANGING DIY SESSION

→ CHATTY WORK-OUT

→ BOOKCASE-REARRANGING PARTY

Make a list of your own favourite friendly things to do!

Jaffles

My mum makes a delicious soup with the flavours of this first recipe. I'm a great believer in putting delicious things into jaffles (or toasties if you prefer) so I invented this spoon-free way to soup it up like Mum!

CHORIZO, POTATO AND TOMATO JAFFLE

A SLOSH OF OLIVE OIL

1 RED ONION, PEELED AND ROUGHLY CHOPPED

1 CLOVE OF GARLIC, PEELED AND DICED

2 LARGE POTATOES, PEELED AND CUT INTO RUSTIC CHUNKS

1 CHORIZO SAUSAGE, DICED

1 RED CAPSICUM, DESEEDED AND DICED ROUGHLY

1 TIN OF CHERRY TOMATOES

SALT AND FRESHLY GROUND PEPPER

GRAINY SANDWICH BREAD, SLICED

FRESH BASIL LEAVES

× Heat the oil in a large frying pan with a lid, and add the onion. Fry until softened, then add the garlic and the potatoes. Stir for a minute and then reduce the heat to low and put the lid on. Cook for 5 minutes over a low heat.

× Now add the red capsicum and cook with the lid on for another 5 minutes, or until the potatoes are soft. Use a potato-masher to mash the potato chunks, then throw in the tomatoes and season with salt and pepper. Put the lid on and cook for another couple of minutes.

× Now you're ready to jaffle!

× Follow my jaffle-making directions at the bottom of the Corn, Bacon and Potato Jaffle recipe, and add some basil to the topping just before you close the jaffle maker.

MAKES ENOUGH FOR ABOUT 8 JAFFLES

CORN, BACON AND POTATO JAFFLE

1 TBSP BUTTER

1 BROWN ONION,
PEELED AND CHOPPED

2 LARGE POTATOES,
PEELED AND DICED

2 RASHERS OF BACON, CHOPPED

200G CORN KERNELS

200G CREAMED CORN

¼ CUP OF MILK

SALT AND FRESHLY GROUND PEPPER

EXTRA BUTTER

GRAINY SANDWICH BREAD, SLICED

× Melt the butter in a large frying pan with a lid. Throw in the onions and potatoes and fry for a minute, making sure they're well coated in butter.

× Put the lid on and cook for 10 minutes over a low heat, checking occasionally to be sure it's not all sticking and burning. When the potatoes are almost tender, add the bacon and stir it all about. Cook for another minute or so.

× Now add the corn kernels, creamed corn and milk. Season with salt and lots of black pepper, and cook for another couple of minutes until it's all thickened up a bit and the potatoes are done.

× Butter a jaffle-maker (not a sandwich press!). Add a bread slice, piling a spoonful or two of the mixture on top of it. Pop a slice of bread on top, close the jaffle-maker and cook for 3–5 minutes, until the bread is toasted golden.

MAKES ENOUGH FOR ABOUT 10 JAFFLES

CHAPTER NINE

Stay home

> Sometimes we
> need to stop so that
> we can assess what
> we're up to.

Retreat. Here's how to do it, in case you've been too busy and forgotten what this means . . .

Lock the front door. Pull the curtains. Switch your phone to silent. Good. Now, head to the kitchen. Put the kettle on. Make some toast or open the cake tin and cut yourself a slice. Make a pot of tea. Put the snacks on a tray. Set off for the lounge room.

Put the tray down. Go to your bedroom. Pull the blinds. Put on your comfiest pyjamas. Add some slippers if it's cold. A pinch of cardigan, even. Great.

Make your bed nicely. Plump the pillows, dim the lights. Now back to the lounge room. Put on your favourite thing to watch. Sit on the couch. Pour a cup of tea. *Sip your tea. Eat your snack. Watch the TV.*

Repeat the part between the asterisks several times.

At this point, you can pull a blanket over yourself and a) read a book b) watch even more telly c) phone a friend or family member you super-love or d) fall asleep. You could even climb into that nicely made bed. How about a hot water bottle? Or if the weather's hot, switch on a breeze.

Next, you could run yourself a bath: make sure it's got something bubbly or fragrant in it. Find a big towel (not one with holes in it), and make sure you have a really good book on hand. Sometimes it's good to light some nice candles. Maybe you want a fancy drink, too? If you're super-sneaky, you could pick some of those flowers that are hanging over your back fence/neighbour's fence and scatter them about. Lock yourself in the bathroom if you share your home with other bathroom-loving types, and have a big soaky, booky, drinky bath.

Take your time. Do girly maintenance things if you want to, but I just like to sloth about – I don't care if I've exfoliated or not, I'm very easy to please. You know, some people even like to eat chocolate in the bath, so you can do that if you want to. I find that it gets a bit melty and gross, but if you have a tried and true way to deal with the warm-water-meets-treat issue then GO for it.

When you get out of the bath, put your pjs back on, by all means. Sloth on.

If you're getting a bit tetchy, you could get dressed, put your headphones in and go for a big walk. You don't actually have to be listening to anything, just put the headphones on – no one will talk to you with headphones on. It's an excellent retreat-extending ruse. While you are ruse-ing, pick up some little treats for yourself. Maybe something good to eat, a new journal, a nice smelly candle[†], a magazine . . . or a new book. Anything that you can forage and take back to your burrow to continue your nice times.

Later, order yourself some home-delivered food, reclaim your couch spot and eat dinner with a blanket. OR make yourself a tower of cheese on toast and several cups of tea. Enjoy them with a crumby front. That's very retreat-y too.

[†] Don't spend a whole bunch on this. Why are smelly candles so pricey?

WHY WE NEED TO RETREAT

I'm not sure about you, but I find that I'm pretty bombarded with all kinds of communication most of the time.

Once I made the grave mistake of syncing Facebook events with my Google calendar, and there were honestly 258 EXTRA things on my to-do list each day. Some of them were from people I didn't even know: 'Lily Languid's Hot Damn Haute Dog Vegan Fiesta For Gluten Intolerant Dogs! Tuesday 7 p.m.! Hoboken.' Um. Thanks but no thanks, Lily.

My email and Facebook messages are not much better. Press releases jostle with announcements of VIP shopping nights for a limited (49 zillion) number of special guests. Lovely emails from people who are interested in my work sit alongside ones that say, 'My lady. Sometimes I find you fluffy. Will you send me fresh corn?' It's quite confusing.

Then there are the in-real-life things I should attend: the work things, the fun things, the friend things, the learning things, the noisy things, the musical things, the inspiring things . . . Gadzooks. It gets a bit much sometimes, and you just need to drop out.

Retreating on a regular basis is really important. Sometimes we need to stop so that we can assess what we're up to, where we're going, who we're going there with. Sometimes we need to slow it down because we're in some kind of fug and can't seem to find a way forward as things swirl noisily about us. Sometimes, we need to retreat because we're run-down and exhausted. We need to head things off at the pass before they get totally stupid and we're a puddle of 'Help!' But my very favourite reason for sneaking away from real life is to have a preventative dose of cosy times. Nothing's wrong exactly, but we know the value of dropping out and snuggling down.

You may not be able to drop out for very long because you have responsibilities or become gripped with inbox terror. But you can most certainly stage a micro-retreat. Drop out for just one day, or for six hours – take what you can get. Much time can be spent huffing and puffing dramatically about how little time we get to ourselves, but if we shift our expectations about the quantity of 'time to ourselves', we can have a marvellous rest-y retreat in a mini dose.

RETREATING WITH FRIENDS

If you have really great friends who don't mind seeing you with unbrushed teeth and bird's-nest hair, you can diversify your retreat by adding extra pals. These kinds of retreats involve leggings-as-pants, cake, something very watchable on telly, Cheezels on fingers, glasses of wine or cups of tea, long chats, stupid photos, dial-in dinners and possibly some bad dancing.

You can retreat with friends at home or you can take things up a notch, plan a road trip and rent a cabin/house/lodge/wigwam. Get amongst the great outdoors. The benefit of this is that not only are you far, far away from the things that vex you, you can slightly less shamefully wear novelty knits, stretchy pants and clown sunglasses.

Retreats away tend to focus more on late-night shenanigans involving glasses of bubbles and terrifyingly competitive games of Scrabble – if you're looking to be physically restored, you may find this wanting. On the other hand, there's a lot to be said for being mentally revived, and a novelty-knitted weekend away with your favourite people is the most restorative tonic known to man. Or lady.

TAKING A SABBATICAL

I love the idea of taking a sabbatical. Can you imagine saying to your people, 'I'm off for a couple of months. I shall travel extensively, write a book and learn new things. I'll wear a headband! Where are my yoga pants?'

Still, for most of us, a sabbatical is not something we have the luxury of entertaining. It's just not on the cards. We have rent and/or mortgages. Our cat needs new shoes. There are people who need us. Life is too busy or pressing or full, and doing something on our own for an extended period is about as likely as me parachuting into a field of gladioli wearing a feather boa: i.e. not likely at all.

If you *are* able to take a sabbatical, then I hope you're reading this book in a yurt in your clogs sipping almond milk with Julia Roberts. Darn you.

Let's not allow our lack of sabbatical opportunities to make us bitter though. We're better than that. Let's take inspiration from the learnt loafing of others, and find ways to build the spirit of the sabbatical into our everyday.

First, let's think about the why. Why take a sabbatical?

→ Rest and rejuvenate
→ Get to know yourself better
→ Consider a change in direction
→ Learn new things
→ Work on a creative project

(This list is very much shorter than my list of why I CAN'T take a sabbatical, by the way!)

Maybe you could tackle some of these sabbatical goals on your solo retreats? Rest and rejuvenate? Tick! Get to know yourself better? Okay! Some of the items might be more fun with friends. Work on a creative project? Friendly! Learn new things? Yep!

The thing is, there's no reason why these sabbatical goals need to be saved up and tucked away for when you've got a spare few months floating around with no pressures and nothing to do. Just do this stuff now. Get going. Concentrate on the things you need to be happier and feel more fulfilled now. Don't wait for permission or circumstance to dictate the life you want. If a gap year won't find you, it's up to you to find your own gaps. Granted, they might be tiny: they might be bite-sized minis, even. But good things really do come in small packages sometimes. Make the most of mini. Take the initiative and jam-pack some of this important stuff into your rest-y days.

PYJAMA DAY MOVIES, ACCORDING TO MY FRIENDS

→ LOVE ACTUALLY

→ EASY A

→ MEAN GIRLS

→ DROP DEAD FRED

→ EDWARD SCISSORHANDS

→ E.T.

→ MOONRISE KINGDOM

→ THE BIG CHILL

→ THE SOUND OF MUSIC

→ THE KING AND I

→ THE BREAKFAST CLUB

→ ANNIE HALL

→ PULP FICTION

→ FARGO

→ TERMS OF ENDEARMENT

→ STEEL MAGNOLIAS

→ TOOTSIE

→ BRING IT ON

→ STEPMOM

→ STAND BY ME

→ LABYRINTH

→ SIXTEEN CANDLES

→ MY NEIGHBOUR TOTORO

→ PRETTY WOMAN

→ THE HELP

→ SENSE AND SENSIBILITY

→ PRETTY IN PINK

→ HIGH FIDELITY

→ DEATH AT A FUNERAL

→ ALMOST FAMOUS

→ REAR WINDOW

→ BEACHES

→ FERRIS BUELLER'S DAY OFF

→ THE GODFATHER SERIES

→ ST ELMO'S FIRE

→ PRIDE AND PREJUDICE

→ THE HARRY POTTER SERIES

→ THE LORD OF THE RINGS SERIES

→ CHARLIE AND THE CHOCOLATE FACTORY

→ THE WIZARD OF OZ

→ GOODFELLAS

→ YOU'VE GOT MAIL

→ ETERNAL SUNSHINE OF
THE SPOTLESS MIND

→ TITANIC

→ TO KILL A MOCKINGBIRD

→ MY FAIR LADY

→ THE NEVERENDING STORY

→ NOTTING HILL

→ PONYO

→ THE SIXTH SENSE

→ HANNAH AND HER SISTERS

→ GREASE

→ NEVER LET ME GO

→ KNOCKED UP

→ HAIRSPRAY

→ FUNNY FACE

→ EAT PRAY LOVE

→ FINDING NEMO

→ BRIDESMAIDS

→ THE BRIDGET JONES
MOVIES

→ THE BLUES BROTHERS

→ DANNY THE CHAMPION
OF THE WORLD

→ STRIPES

→ DIRTY DANCING

→ THE NOTEBOOK

→ TOY STORY

→ LOOK WHO'S TALKING

→ LEGALLY BLONDE

→ FOUR WEDDINGS AND
A FUNERAL

→ MIDNIGHT IN PARIS

→ AMÉLIE

→ CINEMA PARADISO

→ REBECCA OF SUNNYBROOK
FARM

→ IT'S A WONDERFUL LIFE

→ THE PRINCESS BRIDE

→ SINGIN' IN THE RAIN

→ FANTASTIC MR FOX

→ HOWL'S MOVING CASTLE

Even More Toasty Things

I like special things on toast. It's a weakness of mine.

PIP'S MISO, SPINACH AND GREEN OLIVE PESTO

1 CUP OF BABY SPINACH,
WASHED VERY WELL

1 BUNCH OF CORIANDER,
WASHED VERY WELL

½ CUP PITTED GREEN OLIVES

50 G ALMONDS

2 TBSP TOASTED SESAME SEEDS

2 TBSP MISO PASTE

1 TSP SESAME OIL

¼ CUP OF OLIVE OIL

JUICE OF ONE LEMON

FRESHLY GROUND BLACK PEPPER

OPTIONAL: ½ TSP DRIED
CHILLI FLAKES

× Blitz all ingredients in a food processor, store in the fridge and use often!

MAKES ABOUT 1 CUP

RUSTIC ROASTED TOMATO, RED PEPPER AND CASHEW PESTO

½ CUP OF OLIVE OIL, PLUS AN
EXTRA DRIZZLE

1 KG RIPE TOMATOES (OR YOU CAN
USE DRAINED, TINNED TOMATOES)

1 RED CAPSICUM, DESEEDED AND CUT
INTO RUSTIC CHUNKS

1 HEAD OF GARLIC

¾ CUP OF CASHEWS

50 G PARMESAN CHEESE
(I ACTUALLY USED PECORINO)

SEA SALT AND FRESHLY GROUND PEPPER

× Pre-heat the oven to 200 °C. Pour a little oil onto a large oven tray (or you can use two oven trays!) and spread it about. Now tumble on the tomatoes, capsicum and the whole head of garlic.

× Roast in the oven for 30 minutes or until starting to caramelise. Cool.

× In a food processor, blitz the cashews, parmesan and an extra drizzle of olive oil until processed, but still quite lumpy.

× Squeeze the garlic from the roasted head and add that to the food processor, along with the tomatoes and capsicum, a pinch of sea salt and some ground black pepper. Process until combined and pesto-y.

MAKES ABOUT 2 CUPS

POTATO CURRY

I invented this dish when my eldest was a wee baby. It's really the super-goodness! I love it on toast, but you can also pile it into a soft roll with some relish and rocket for a totally winning portable lunch. I prefer it cold on hot toast, personally!

1 KG OF NICE POTATOES, PEELED AND CUT INTO RUSTIC CUBES

2 TBSP VEGETABLE OR OLIVE OIL

2 LARGE ONIONS, ROUGHLY CHOPPED

2 CLOVES OF GARLIC, SMASHED AND CHOPPED UP

2.5 CM OF FRESH GINGER, GRATED OR CHOPPED FINELY

1 TBSP CURRY POWDER

1 TBSP SOY SAUCE

1 CUP OF WATER

200 G FROZEN PEAS

SALT AND FRESHLY GROUND PEPPER

FRESH CORIANDER

FRESH MINT, CHOPPED

NICE BREAD FOR TOASTING

× In a large saucepan of water, boil the potatoes until they're almost tender.

× While they're boiling, heat the oil in a large frying pan and sauté the onion until golden – stir it often and make sure it doesn't burn. When it's nice and golden and catching a bit on the bottom of the pan, throw in the garlic and ginger and stir for 30 seconds. Then add the almost-cooked potatoes and toss or stir to combine all ingredients in the pan.

× Next, mix the curry powder, soy sauce and water and pour the mixture into the pan over the potatoes. Mix and fry well.

× Add the peas, and keep simmering and tossing until the liquid has reduced – it's meant to be a dry-ish curry.

× Season well with salt and pepper, garnish with coriander and serve hot or cold on toast.

SERVES 6

CHAPTER TEN

Do your work!

HOW TO DO GOOD WORK

WORK. Look at that word. Does it make you shudder? Does it grip your stomach with a handful of angst? It's kind of a sweary word, right? It doesn't seem very positive or like something we'd want to do.

Work. Hard work. Work–life balance. Workaholic. Argh!

I think we need to reclaim work as a vital, exciting metier, full of promise, lessons and growth. Work is often referred to as something to battle with, something to be overcome or tamed or endured. But considering we spend a huge amount of our time working, surely it's a better idea to find ways to embrace work?

What about good work, work it out, workable? Better!

Work gives us purpose, teaches us discipline, helps us keep a roof over our heads, allows us to learn and grow, forces us to challenge ourselves, provides us with insight into who we are and what we like and don't like. It provides us with all sorts of opportunities to assess ourselves and our lives, to set goals, and to pursue skills and ideas we wouldn't otherwise be exposed to.

Work unites us with other people too, as we chase common goals of money and/or meaning in different ways.

We're all programmed to work most of our adult lives, retiring at sixty-five, when we're meant to spend our twilight years snipping roses and reading all the books we never had time for when we were working. The wisdom of this anti-work retirement focus is questionable. Who says that not working is the ideal? Why is work, the very thing that gives us so much purpose, the enemy?

Shift yourself out of the 'work=enemy' mindset. Shake it up and step into the 'work=love' gang. Embrace and make the best of the work you do. Resisting something that's such a big part of your life is not only exhausting, it's counterproductive. You'll spend so much time enduring that you'll stop yourself from excelling. Why not shift things a little, and aim at doing the work you love? Surely that's more meaningful than working towards a goal of ultimately doing nothing?

Not only does this shift encourage you to stay healthy so you can cram in all the good bits without a 'finish line' in mind, but retiring later has been proven to help prevent dementia (and depression!). Purpose, discipline and meaning keep us well. We can't embrace these shifted goalposts without embracing work!

Perhaps you're not even thinking about that olde worlde time in your life: perhaps you're WAY too youthful for that? Maybe, though, you spend a lot of time focussing on weekends, home time, breaks and sick days instead? I get that those times are great (except the sick days), but don't do that! You're disengaging from your life and robbing yourself of opportunities to acquire new skills or learn new stuff. Pulling away from work is a trap. Stepping up and committing is a much better idea, and the key to finding purpose and meaning and getting things done. Positivity, productivity and fronting up with an open mind and a keen will to do well reaps big rewards. So do that. Yep.

Shake it up
and step into the
'work=love' gang.

LEARN TO SAY 'YEP!'

We spend a lot of time assessing where we fit in, what's okay, what we're entitled to, what our rights are, what we deserve. I think this is great. But sometimes I think it's really easy to miss opportunities and avoid challenges if we're too busy thinking about the whys and wherefores, the risks and the problems, the workflow, the 'fit', whether this is 'our job'. Sometimes, it's really great to say, 'Sure! I'll do that!' and see where it leads. Sometimes it's good to say 'Yes!'

A lot of the time we learn by doing, and achieve our greatest wins by having a go and seeing what happens. There are all kinds of reasons *not* to do things, but some of them involve us getting in our own way, making excuses or taking the easy option. Do you think people who achieve great or satisfying things take the easy option? No, they do not. Learn to say 'YEP!' at least some of the time. Nod your head as you do it. Smile, even. Have a crack.

What are you passionate about?

DO YOUR BEST AT WHATEVER JOB YOU HAVE

You never know what benefits will come from the work that you do.
Maybe it's something tangible like finishing a god-awful project and feeling
the relief of moving on. Maybe it's better than that: maybe it's a successful
project and you can celebrate your win. Perhaps your gain is a fresh
perspective provided by working on something difficult or lengthy. That
might be a new way of looking at yourself, a new approach to collaboration,
or even a new way of tackling daunting tasks. You won't know what you're
capable of and what the gains will be if you don't try your best.

When I'm working, I always look back over what I've done and think,
'What can I do to make this EVEN better?' I'm not the sort of person to
go through the motions and complete the task. Even if the job at hand is
something I'm not too keen on, I figure a) it's got my name attached to it,
so I'd better make it good! and b) what's the point of just enduring it when
I could turn it around and make something good happen?!

'What can I do to make this even better?' It's a great rule of thumb,
because a lot of people coast through life and do just enough to get by.
The people who go the extra mile are noticeable, not just for their great
work, but for their sparkly, unicorn attitude too. People like to work with
the extra-milers, because they're positive and productive. They tend to get
more work too . . . because they're positive and productive. You can be an
extra-miler (aka sparkly unicorn) or you can be a coaster. It's up to you.

If you are a coaster, the person who does just enough, who's watching
the clock, thinking about who stole their pot of yoghurt from the tea-
room fridge, you might be missing all kinds of opportunities to do better
work and feel awesome about yourself. Also, you might not get offered
exciting projects, social engagements or promotions, because you've got
your head in the bin trying to match the lipstick on a discarded yoghurty
spoon to a co-worker.

Don't always be trying to escape from your work. Find ways to be
part of the bigger picture. Don't be a coaster. Go the extra mile.

. . . gardens are not made
by singing: 'Oh, how beautiful!'
and sitting in the shade.

RUDYARD KIPLING,
'THE GLORY OF THE GARDEN'

FINDING 'YOUR' WORK VS HATING YOUR JOB

Perhaps you don't like your job? I think a huge portion of the population is in this regrettable boat. I've been there too. I've had many jobs that I really wasn't keen on, so don't think I'm preaching from some lofty, amazing-jobbed heights. I've been in the trenches: I know how muddy it is and what a battle it can seem.

I think if you hate your job you have to get another. Don't scoff. It may not be immediately practical, but it's totally true. You cannot spend your life doing a job that makes you sad/angry/crazy. It's your duty, as a human being, to find something more meaningful for you. That's what you deserve. Come over here, let's hug it out. Now, find a way out of that job.

Gone are the days when people had one or two jobs in their lifetime. Our workforce is more fluid now. We're working in a variety of contract, permanent, intern, volunteer, part-time or casual positions. We dip in and out of work when we have children or travel or study. It's not a clear path, and there are plenty of opportunities to divert from the road you're on.

Work is what you make it, if you're in a position to make it work for you. Perhaps financial pressures or other responsibilities mean that you can't make a big change right now? That's okay. Start implementing smaller changes. Go step by baby step. Write down where you think you want to be and where you are now, and start hatching an escape plan, be it lowering your overheads, doing online study, arranging child care or moving interstate or further afield.

Think hard about what 'your' work might be. What are you passionate about? What has meaning for you? What are you especially interested in? What do you want to be when you grow up?!

When I was little, I wanted to be a writer. Along the way, though, I got lost and became a supermarket cashier, a nanny, a cook, a café owner, and a fashion buyer. I sat myself down one day and had a stern word with me. I brought up the dream of being a writer, dragged it back out into the light of day and turned the possibility over again. Then I marched upstairs and emailed a publisher with an idea for a book. They said yes; I wrote a book. I am now a writer. Shazam.

Of course dreams aren't always achieved by the mere act of asking for them. The important thing is to take steps towards them. Don't tread water, find little ways to move ahead if a big move doesn't seem possible yet. Scale your expectation of change down a little. Sometimes small movements can have a significant impact. Think about that chaos theory with the butterfly and the typhoon: 'It has been said that something as small as the flutter of a butterfly's wing can ultimately cause a typhoon halfway around the world.' I'm thinking you don't want a typhoon, but change begets change, so make some purposeful, regular movement in the direction you want to go. If you want some movement, move something.

ACTIVITY

Make a go-to list of
rad people and
rad reading.

FIND MENTORS AND HEROES,
GATHER INFORMATION AND READ HEAPS

You might be really awesome, but there are other awesome people out there too! Don't exist in a bubble and shut yourself away from influences. Find people you admire and read their work. Or read about them. Or look at pictures of their work.

Immerse yourself in the brilliance of others, their work practices, their theories. Read about how they pace their day, how they stay inspired, their failures and successes. Use their stories as motivation for your own. Take note of how they pushed through difficulties, what setbacks they overcame, how they come up with ideas, who inspires them. Take their work ethic as inspiration for yours.

Find positive work role models, instead of tuning into the usual 'TGIF' chorus. Gather a list of your kind of rad people – maybe they're artists or musicians, scientists or writers? Make seeking rad people part of your homework. Look for them every day and make notes about why you're excited by the work or the things they do.

Visit the big newspaper and opinion sites. Read the news! Click on the science or health or history section. Tune into new, current information and educate yourself. I know a lot of people who choose their reading specifically to filter out what's really going on in the world, and I totally understand how comforting that can feel. But if you want to be relevant and aware and wide-awake, you need to spend a little bit of time in the real world.

Smart, switched-on, brainy people are ready to work and are rewarding to work with. If you want the kind of job that attracts that sort of person, you really need to be that kind of person.

Learn from others, look for mentors and heroes, stay relevant and be switched on.

PRODUCTIVITY AND OUR OBSESSION WITH
WORK-LIFE BALANCE

What is this thing called work–life balance? I understand the need to have enough 'life' time, so that you don't poke someone in the eye out of sheer frustration during your 'work' time. But I really think we need a big shake-up on this issue.

Work–life balance is a way to take stock of how we're feeling about our professional and personal endeavours. It's also a way to measure ourselves and feel dissatisfied with our performance. Don't you think it's weird that we build measures into our life that don't tend to be very helpful? When we spend so much time working in or out of the home, measuring work–life balance keeps us in a constant state of resistance. We tend to resist the work time, trying to grasp at the life time. And when we're having the life time, we're feeling morose because we see the work time on the distant horizon. Gah. If we just settled into our lives and let the work thing and the life thing happen without getting out the measure, we'd be SO MUCH HAPPIER! I think there are better ways to approach this kind of taking stock (see Taking Stock list in chapter 4).

I think we need to redefine work–life balance. I'm not a fan. I think it compartmentalises life in an impossible way and sets us up for failure. So let's assume instead that work and life are intertwined. Work and life will converge. They're not two separate ends of a seesaw, taking turns at being served up. They are two important parts of life that mesh together and fill our days. When you have a job you don't like, the life part of the work–life equation is the thing you long for. When you have a job you love, the life part becomes less defined, as you're much happier to let the lines blur a little. So rather than trying to make the work part as separate as possible (because it's too demanding, exhausting, annoying), figure out ways to make the work part more rewarding.

If you can't make work more rewarding (because you work with insanely snotty people or because you can't possibly be cheery about cleaning your 18 930 440 gazillionth toilet or because you're plucking juice-soaked crackers from down the back of the car seat), then work out ways to build more rewards into your day. Seize some happy moments.

This might mean getting up an hour earlier to do something you love. It might mean using your lunch break to listen to podcasts, take photos, lie in the park, go to the library, draw or read a really amazing book. Perhaps it means looking VERY MUCH FORWARD to your commute because you can listen to Fleetwood Mac all the way to work. Or it could mean meeting a pal for lunch every single Wednesday, or buying someone random in the office a cake once a week.

You have to shift the focus from what you think you're missing out on to what you can achieve. You have to create your own balance by seizing opportunities where you can to do the things that mean something to you.

The work you do is part of your life. Your life is your work. It's all okay.

WORK AND PROCRASTINATION

I'm not even sure why this word 'procrastination' exists. Granted, I know what it means, but it seems to have such a negative connotation, no? It really shouldn't. That's so judgy-pants. Procrastination is a negative label for a positive state. Because procrastination can be all kinds of other things in disguise.

Procrastinating? Maybe you just need a bit of nuff-nuff time to defrag? That's relaxation or self-preservation, not procrastination.

Procrastinating? Maybe it's time clicking around on the internet, looking at interesting things. That's inspiration and research, not procrastination.

Procrastinating? Maybe it's doing the washing instead of finishing a proposal? That's shifting gears, but it's not procrastination.

Procrastinating? Maybe it's making a cup of tea instead of starting work? That's preparation, not procrastination.

I think we tend to beat ourselves up a bit over so-called idle time. And I think that this time is neither idle or procrastinate-y. I think so-called skiving off is actually more about readiness, research, inspiration and relaxation. None of these are bad things, and all will prepare you better for the work or play you're aiming to do.

If we constantly cast 'downtime' and 'procrastination' as the productivity and happiness villains, we're acting nuts and selling ourselves short. Think of it like this: an athlete doesn't constantly train at their very best level. There are all kinds of strengthening and stretching exercises and things to build their tolerance and stamina so they can be the best. They're not just running/swimming/anvil-chucking at full bore all the time. Instead, they're layering their efforts, making sure they're looking after their body and mind, and optimising their health and life in varied ways.

So let's take a leaf from those sporty people. Let's approach life as creative athletes, allow ourselves warm-ups, inspiration junkets, cups of tea and gear-switches. We really, truly need to do those things to keep ourselves on track, to loosen up our brains, to ignite clever sparks and to short-circuit monotony.

I think the seeds of procrastination – the distracted feeling that rolls in like a fog – is just longing for something else. It's a cry for help. It means we need to change gears, get up and do something different; give ourselves a time-out. I think our brains and bodies know just when we need to do this. And we know just the thing that's going to reset us and get us back on track to a better day.

We need to stop avoiding procrastination and call it something less judgemental. Maybe you want to call it Beryl? That's fine with me. Grab onto Beryl. Hold her tight and make her a cup of tea.

Own these times when you need to shift gears or shift your brain to something new. Know that they're the pick-me-ups that fortify and refresh you, set you on a new path and steer you away from idea-killing boredom. Find your own system for making the most of circuit-breaking moments, and use them for your own happy-making tasks. Give yourself permission, when you feel the fog rolling in, to seize the moment and do something you really love (even if it's only for ten or fifteen minutes!).

Write a list of your favourite flowers. Watch some YouTube clips of people you love speaking about things that interest you. Write a poem. Read a poem. Make yourself something delicious to eat. Read a chapter of a good book. Write a letter to your granny. Do some yoga. Go for a walk. Meditate.

Instead of trying to force yourself to stay on task, allow yourself a diversion. Put some time in to refresh yourself. Take it seriously and make a meal of it. You'll feel better. You'll be better. Then get back to work with a fresh mindset.

TIPS FOR DOING GOOD WORK

→ WHEN YOU THINK YOU'VE FINISHED SOMETHING, ASK
  THIS: 'I'VE DONE IT, BUT IS IT THE BEST I CAN DO?'
  IF THE ANSWER IS 'NO', KEEP WORKING.

→ FIND THE PURPOSE IN YOUR WORK AND LET THAT GUIDE
  YOU THROUGH.

→ IF YOUR WORK ISN'T THAT INTERESTING TO YOU, BUT
  HELPS KEEP A ROOF OVER YOUR HEAD, THAT'S AS GOOD
  A PURPOSE AS ANY! (BUILD CREATIVE INSPIRATION INTO
  OTHER AREAS OF YOUR LIFE AND CONSIDER HATCHING
  AN ESCAPE PLAN.)

→ DON'T GIVE UP. FORGET THE 'WHEN IT STOPS BEING
  FUN, STOP' IDEA. SOME OF THE BIGGEST GAINS COME
  FROM PUSHING THROUGH YOUR COMFORT ZONE. KEEP
  GOING!

→ IF YOU'RE FEELING OVERWHELMED, DON'T FREAK OUT.
  WRITE A WORK PLAN AND BREAK YOUR TASKS DOWN INTO
  SMALLER, BITE-SIZED, MANAGEABLE PIECES. REMEMBER,
  BIRD BY BIRD!

→ ALLOW DOWNTIME!

→ GET AHEAD. AT THE END OF YOUR DAY, WRITE A
  SHORT LIST OF THE THINGS YOU'LL WORK ON TOMORROW,
  THEN LEAVE THEM TILL TOMORROW. TAKE A BREAK AND
  RECHARGE. DO SOME NON-WORKY STUFF.

→ THE KEY TO PRODUCTIVITY IS STARTING. GET STARTED,
  EVEN IF YOU HAVE TO PUSH YOURSELF. JUST GET ON
  WITH IT!

→ LOOK TO YOUR MENTORS AND HEROES WHEN YOU'RE STUCK
  FOR INSPIRATION.

→ IF YOU'RE FEELING LIKE YOU'RE IN A FUG, CHANGE
  SOMETHING: GO FOR A WALK, MAKE A PHONE CALL, READ
  SOMETHING INTERESTING. DON'T DWELL ON THE PROBLEM;
  RATHER, SHAKE UP YOUR ROUTINE/BRAIN TO FIND A
  FRESH SOLUTION WITHOUT OVERTHINKING THINGS.

Best Chicken Sandwiches

These are my famous party sandwiches. They're based on the sandwiches we used to make at a catering company I once worked for, but I have fancied them up to suit me.

1 ROAST CHICKEN,
MEAT AND SKIN REMOVED

2 STICKS OF CELERY, DICED

HANDFUL OF ROASTED ALMONDS,
CHOPPED

¼ CUP OF MAYONNAISE

¼ CUP OF SOUR CREAM

½ CUP OF COLD, COOKED PEAS

HANDFUL OF MINT,
TORN INTO LITTLE PIECES

JUICE OF HALF A LEMON

A GOOD SHAKE OF TABASCO SAUCE

SALT AND FRESHLY GROUND PEPPER

1 LOAF OF NICE BROWN BREAD

× Mix all the ingredients together to form a nice creamy mix. Add more mayo if you are that sort of person. Season to taste with pepper and salt and spread onto brown bread.

× You can add avocado or baby spinach if you like. Pea shoots are lovely too!

MAKES ENOUGH FOR 6 HUNGRY PEOPLE

CHAPTER ELEVEN

Earn some badges

This is the part of the book where I get a bit whimsical. I know. It had to happen, right? If you know me, you'll know I'm quite whimsical in general. I've been working very hard to keep the whimsy under control for most of this book: I didn't want the whimsy to detract from the dead-serious-important things I had to say. I sort of sprinkled it sparingly as needed, rather than tipping it on with abandon as per, well, me.

But we're at the last chapter and I need to cut loose. I'm not totally unicorn-ing out with a complete cuteness overload, though – I'm applying a quite-serious-important version of whimsy instead.

At first glance this badge plan seems a little bit cutesy, but actually it's a totally clever plan to keep you on track, focussed, entertained and accountable, with a nod to childhood thrown in. Let's go.

ABOUT THE BADGES

This badge system is a) cute and b) helpful. We've covered a lot of stuff together in this book, and I wanted to think of a way to pull it all together into some kind of action plan. With badges. Because badges are rad. Badges were, in fact, the only reason I joined the Brownies, but that's another story.

Badges seem like a positive, practical and visual way to create a kind of 'Nice Life Master Plan' and celebrate achievements. Think of them as a method of pulling ourselves out of that foggy day-to-day survival mode we often find ourselves in and set us firmly down in front of possibility.

LOOK AT THAT WORD: ---> POSSIBILITY <----

What kind of possibility am I talking about? Well, the possibility that we can improve our lives in simple, achievable, logical ways without a huge amount of effort. The possibility that small, consistent changes can lead to big gains. The possibility that if we brush the familiar cobwebs out of the corners of our life we'll catch a glimpse of something better. The possibility that things that seem like huge hurdles might be less of a problem that we think.

There are other possibilities too. The kind of possibility that lies in easy-peasy actions like changing your routine, getting a bit healthier, not rolling your eyes at your mum, saying yes to things you might not usually, talking kindly to yourself, taking the first steps towards something you really want to do, staying home instead of going places you hate, learning from other rad people, or even just liking who you are. Actually, ESPECIALLY liking who you are.

In the end, a lot of this stuff boils down to self-acceptance: knowing that who you are is really more than okay. Knowing that you – with your history and your flaws and your ace bits and your worries and your quirks and your mess-ups and your triumphs – you are really jam-packed with everything you need to be.

You just need to think about the bits you want to tinker with and find little (or big) ways to get tweaking every day. (In a non-creepy way. Because that sounded a bit sexy/weird, as if it involved nipples or the like. I don't think it does . . . Maybe it does for some people; I don't like to judge.)

To clarify, what I am saying is, you just need to make the most of you.

Do what you can each day. Do your best, with an eye to taking stock and improving where you feel you need to.

If you have days when you feel like sitting on the couch and eating Fruit Chews (I do!) while you watch all the episodes of *Breaking Bad* or *Hart of Dixie*, know that sometimes that's a part of looking after yourself. Don't think that all is lost. Just know that it was that kind of day. Nice one. No biggie. Move on. Don't let that derail your efforts.

Similarly, when you have days where you get things done, two things or twenty-two things, then know it was THAT kind of day. Fist bump! Keep doing that.

If you need a plan to keep you on track, the badges are that plan. Choose a few or choose them all. I've carefully devised thirteen based on all the bits of this book – one for each month plus an extra . . . a baker's dozen!

You can download the badges from my blog (meetmeatmikes. com) and print them out to stick on the fridge or in a notebook. Or you can just come back to page 170 and mark them off triumphantly as you work your way through.

Badge along for the entire year if you like. Feel free not to, as well. Feel free to create your own badge ideas and tasks, or work on a few for longer than a month each. Work on them for a lifetime if you like. Or just now and again. Do with this what you will. We're really not as organised as the Brownies or Guides or Camp Fire Girls, are we? Navigate this in your own way. That would be best.

Here are the badges and tasks.

1. FAMILY

Set yourself three tasks to celebrate or improve family life. They could be things like 'Ring Nanna every week', 'Remember to breathe when Dad brings up those stories about skinny-dipping when I was six' or 'Do not drink six glasses of wine at each family gathering'. You know the good bits and less good bits in your family. Work out what's irking you and get to work on dealing with those things in the best way you can. Maybe you can't fix things or even control how they turn out, but you get points for showing up, especially if things are particularly difficult with some family types. Nice work. Phew.

2. FRIENDS

Set yourself three really fun things to do with your pals. You can consult my list on page 129 or you can make up your own tasks. I don't tend to include any extreme sports/height-related things in my writing, but if you want to throw in some parasailing or hot air ballooning or monster truck racing, go nuts. It's also okay if your tasks involve quiet times with friends, just one friend or a larger, good bunch.

3. HEALTH

Think of three ways you can improve your health and wellbeing. Do each of those things for at least 21 days. Apparently that's how long it takes to form a habit, so go for a 21-day run of success. When you get to the 21-day mark, make a note of how you felt before and after. (You can do this in the notes section on your phone or write in an ACTUAL journal, it's up to you!) You can track your progress through the entire period if you're the studious kind. Mark every 21 days with a gold star. Keep going!

4. TRAVEL

Take a trip. We're all quite busy, so your trip might only be to the outer suburbs of your city or a nearby town. I get that. It's okay. Move out of your usual hood and go somewhere fresh and new. Take photos. Create memories. Be extra clever and take a friend or family member to get a head start on THAT badge as well. Later, notice how much fun it is and make a date to do it again soon.

5. FIX-IT

Think about the Fix-it Shop and its amazing powers of improvement. How can you resist the possibility that restoring, repairing or reviving something might pay dividends in other ways? I'm sure you can't, so do that. Fix three things. Perhaps they're the messy fridge or leaky tap kind of things. Maybe they are bigger things like moving to a better neighbourhood, going to the doctor about those dark days or dealing with something hugely annoying like an accountant or insurance or the like. Whatever it is, fix three things, big or small. Then keep fixing things as often as you can.

6. HERO

Choose someone famous or accomplished or inspiring and STUDY them – totally geek out. Fangirl it, as Tavi Gevinson says. Immerse yourself in all the bits of them that you find interesting. Make a scrapbook. Start a Tumblr about them. Read their books or listen to their music or look at their art. Whoever you choose, dig deep and find out what makes them tick. Connect the dots too, and work out WHY you're so into them. Think about the parallels between you and them. Soak them up and let the ace-ness inspire you and spill over into your life. (NB: do not stalk people, that's not what I mean!)

7. SKILL

Learn a new skill. You don't have to master it, but begin to learn something new and commit to some level of success. French? Watercolour painting? Breaststroke? Needlepoint? The choice is yours. Search your local adult education centre for courses you might like, learn from a neighbour or enlist the help of a patient friend. One new skill = one badge. You might want to keep learning new things or perhaps to delve even deeper into the first thing you chose. Whichever it is, keep learning!

8. HISTORY

Remember when we did the 'Write your own bio' exercise? The history badge is about taking stock of your whole life. Don't freak out: it's a sort of synopsis rather than the Complete Works of You. There are all kinds of ways you could do this: online with images in a private gallery just for you, in a scrapbook or diary, or in audio/video form. Make a timeline of who you are, where you've been and what you've achieved. Use your original bio as the framework and delve a bit deeper, recounting anecdotes or adding images. You don't have to show this to anyone, but it's a great way of collating and celebrating the history of YOU! That earns you this badge. Keep adding to your history as you do new, great stuff.

9. WORK

Improve three things at work. Perhaps it's just dealing with the foreboding sense you get when you're nearly at the office (by building in a pre-work treat!). Maybe it's bigger than that – chasing a promotion or looking further afield for more suitable work. It might be taking in some home-baked treats one day a week, or starting a charitable project with your workmates, or shifting your whole attitude. Think about what your three things are and do those. Then get a badge! Win!

10. MAKE

Making things makes things better. It just does. Amy Krouse Rosenthal made a film called just that (*Making Things Makes Things Better*). Clare Bowditch wrote a song about it ('Amazing Life'). I've spent a lot of my adult life knowing that making stuff is not only fun, it connects you to other people, it honours skills that link back to your childhood and others in your family, it transports you into some kind of meditative, clever-feeling, joyful state AND you get a thing at the end of it too. To earn your Make badge, you need to make three things. They can be long and involved makings or speedy-quick. It's totally up to you. Use your head and heart to hatch a plan and use your hands to see it through. Make three things.

11. LOAF

Tee-hee. Loaf. I like this one, because it makes me think of bread. I love bread! You might have fathomed by now that I try not to eat too much bread. Loafing, in the resting/relaxing sense of the word, is just the same . . . If you're like me, you probably try not to do it too much. It's sad really. We tend to demonise time spent 'doing nothing' because we live in this culture of busy. We feel terrible if we 'waste time', but often a bit of mindless lolling about is just the thing we need to restore ourselves and gather energy. Dedicate ONE WHOLE DAY to loafing. That wins you this badge. And don't feel bad afterwards. Give yourself some downtime (even if it's gluten- or wheat-free!).

12. DETECTIVE

This is a goodie. Look for clues. Remember when we talked about clues as happiness and creativity prompts? I want you to imagine Elvis Costello is playing in your head when you're out and about, or watching a movie, or reading a book, or looking at a really interesting blog. I want you to look for clues: look for the things that pique your interest and give you ideas, that make you want to learn, know, do, see or live more. And I want you to write those things down and read them back often. If you start a clue-noting journal, you can earn this badge.

13. DREAM

Here's the thing. It's wonderful to get a handle on life, Nice Times, happiness in the here and now. That is so great. I can't even tell you how great. It's TOTALLY GREAT. Worthy of capitals even. BUT you have to have goals. You have to have wonderings. You have to have DREAMS. You have to think about the fact that there's more you want to do. Write down three MORES: three DREAMS. Three things that excite you, that you really want to do, even if those things seem totally out of reach. Write them down and put them in an envelope, and put that envelope somewhere safe. The place where you keep your important documents like tickets to concerts and passports and things would be PERFECT. To earn this badge, do that. And then look in the envelope sometimes and have a think about the dreams. Add any extra ones that might pop up. If the envelope gets too bunchy, you can upgrade to a nice box or something . . . It's always good to make room for extra dreams.

Craft projects

FUZZY FEELINGS POMPOM RUG

Sometimes you just need something adorable and cosy to look at/make. This rug is a woolly labour of love, but totally worth it!

YOU NEED:

×   80 OR SO POMPOMS

×   A PIECE OF HESSIAN MEASURING 120 CM × 100 CM

×   A 50 G BALL OF YARN TO MATCH YOUR HESSIAN

×   A WOOL NEEDLE

×   SCISSORS

×   A BIT OF SPARE TIME

NB: The rug will end up a bit smaller than the piece of hessian, because we need to leave some excess and hem it neatly at the end.

LET'S MAKE IT:

1. Start sewing the pompoms onto the hessian. I started at one end and worked my way down, leaving around 5 cm excess hessian for hemming later.

2. To sew a pompom into place, stitch a couple of 'anchoring' stitches into the hessian, making sure to leave a 'tail' of yarn about 10 cm long. Then, firmly sew the pompom into position with at least 10 firm stitches. Make sure it's sewn on tightly. Cut your yarn and tie a couple of very firm knots on the underside of your hessian to secure it nicely. Ta-dah! One pompom down! 79 or so to go!

3. Repeat this process for all of your pompoms, making sure that each pompom is snuggled up closely to the next. It will take a while to stitch them all on, so perhaps put a box set of something ace on the TV and settle in for the day with a pot of tea and some nice biscuits.

4. Once you've sewn on all the pompoms, or the rug is as big as you like, trim the edges of the hessian to within 3 cm of the pompoms (do the best you can, as pompoms don't make a very straight edge!)

5. With the pompom side of your rug facing up, tuck that trimmed edge neatly under so that the fold is concealed by the pompoms. We don't want to see that fold. Pin the tucked-under edge into place if you like, or just hold in place and neatly blanket-stitch along the fold with your yarn and wool needle to make a tidy finish. This hem will stop your rug from fraying and make it look super-profesh.

6. When you have neatly blanket-stitched each side of the rug, trim all your loose yarn ends neatly. This will ensure that the back of the rug looks nice.

7. Now flip your new rug over, straighten up your pompoms and marvel at your woolly cleverness!

HOW TO MAKE A POMPOM

If you think pompom-making takes an age, you've got another thing coming! Here's a speedy way to pompom. It takes ten minutes from go to whoa . . . unless you fall asleep.

YOU NEED:

× POMPOM TEMPLATE (SEE PAGE 177)

× THICKISH CARDBOARD (A CEREAL BOX WOULD DO)

× SOME ODDMENTS OF YARN

× SCISSORS

× WHITE PAPER

LET'S MAKE IT:

1. Trace the template onto some white paper, then cut out two identical cardboard circles using the paper template as a guide.

2. Cut a 70 cm or so length of yarn and set aside.

3. Place your cut-out circles on top of each other with the template atop them (three circles in total!). Match the curved edges neatly.

4. Cut a short line from the outer edge of the circle to the small circle, using the dotted line as a guide.

5. Cut out the entire centre circle using the circle on the template as your guide. Cut a narrow notch from the outer circle edge to the inner circle.

6. Start wrapping your yarn around, as close to the notch you cut as possible, without it slipping off the notched edge. You can use one colour or keep changing colours.

7. Put the radio on, sing along, sip tea, phone a friend (use speakerphone!).

8. Keep wrapping your yarn all the way around the circles until the middle is getting snug with yarn. Then stop wrapping and snip your yarn from its ball with a 50 cm tail.

9. Here's the mildly tricky bit: cut your yarn away from the template and cardboard by snipping the outermost wrapped edge. Just shimmy your scissors carefully in between the yarn and cardboard and snip all the way around as close to the outer circle edge as possible. (Takes a bit of juggling!) Keep your hand on top of the yarn and pompom sandwich as you do, so it all stays put. You might have to hack a bit, but just do your best to keep everything in place.

10. Now, while you balance the whole pompom sandwich, hand atop it all, wrap the 70 cm length of yarn you cut earlier between the two cardboard circles, pulling it tight and giving it a good knotting. Phew. It's all secure now. Wrap and knot a couple of extra times for good measure.

11. Tie the two free long bits of yarn together in a couple of knots to pull the pompom in securely.

12. Remove the cardboard circles carefully. Plump it out cutely: ta-dah! A pompom!

HELLO

POMPOM

IT'S OBLONG STORY:
CROCHETED GRANNY RECTANGLE BLANKET

If you've ever made a granny square before, you'll easily be able to make this. It's the same idea, just made from an elongated rectangle base and grown round by round. This is a cute thing to learn how to do, because you can make big rectangles without having to stitch squares together. You could make a cot blanket in a weekend quite easily, or a pet blanket in a day!

YOU NEED:

× ODDMENTS OF YARN OR 6 × 50G BALLS FOR A LAP BLANKET

× A 3.5MM CROCHET HOOK

× YARN NEEDLE WITH A LARGE EYE

× SCISSORS

LET'S MAKE IT:

1. Foundation: Chain 23 stitches.

Make the first side of the rectangle:

2. Treble two into the third chain from hook.
3. Chain one.
4. Skip two stitches.
5. Treble three into the next stitch. Chain one. Skip two.
6. Repeat step 5 five more times.

Make the corners' rectangle base:

7. Treble three into the final stitch – corner one.
8. Chain three.
9. Treble three into the same stitch as before – end of rectangle.
10. Chain three.
11. Treble three once more into the same stitch as before – corner two.
12. Chain one.

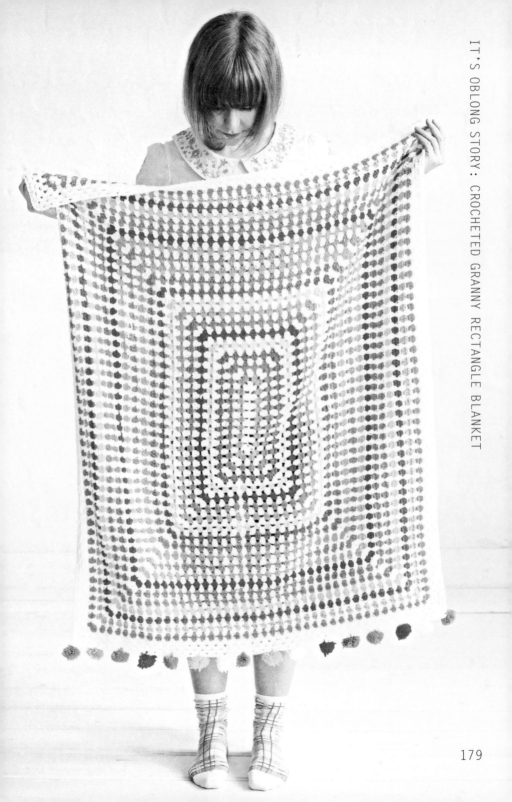

Complete the other side of the rectangle base:

13. Treble three into the stitch opposite – the same stitch you treble clustered in for the other side. It will be quite easy, as the stitch is stretched out now! Chain one.
14. Repeat step 13 five more times, matching the clusters to those you crocheted on the other side of the foundation chain.

Make the other corners of the rectangle:

15. Treble three into the bottom of the very first cluster you made.
16. Chain three.
17. Treble three into the same spot as before.
18. Chain two.
19. Slip-stitch into the top of the very first cluster you made to close the rectangle.
20. Tie off your yarn with a long tail for weaving or crocheting in later.
21. Tie on the next coloured yarn. Just tie it in one of the one chain 'gaps' in the middle of the rectangle's side.
22. Chain up three (counts as one treble stitch!).
23. Treble twice into the gap below.
24. Chain one. Treble three times into the next gap. Chain one.
25. Repeat step 24 until you approach the corner.
26. Treble three into the corner gap in the row below. Chain three. Treble three back into the same corner gap. Chain one.
27. Crochet the other corner in the same way. Then crochet the other side as you did the first. When you get to the corner again: treble three into the corner gap in the row below. Chain three. Treble three back into the same corner gap. Chain one.
28. Repeat for the other corner, then continue along the side until you run out of 'gaps' in the row below. Slip-stitch into the top right stitch of the very first treble cluster you made in this 'round' and fasten off.

How to continue on crocheting each 'round':

29. Crochet the long sides of the rectangle: Tie on your new yarn colour in any side 'gap'. Chain up three. Treble twice into the gap below. Chain one.

30. Treble three into the next gap in the row below. Chain one. Treble three into the next gap along in the row below. Chain one.

31. Repeat the step 30 pattern until you reach the corner (then repeat the corner instructions!).

Crochet the corners of the rectangle:

32. Treble three into the corner gap in the row below. Chain three. Treble three back into the same corner gap. Chain one.

Crochet the shorter ends of the rectangle:

33. The ends of the rectangle will get wider with each round, just crochet into the gaps as you did for each side. You only need to get fancy at the corners.

34. Change colour as you like, after each row or not. Your blanket will grow quickly and you can make it whatever size suits you!

35. Crochet over loose ends to hide the yarn, or snip a 30 cm length before you fasten off and use a yarn needle to neatly weave the yarn between the matching stitches a few times, then snip carefully close to your work and fasten off.

ATTACK THE BLOCK BLANKET

Crocheted blankets can be quite fussy, which is why I super-love this simple design. You can take this idea and choose your own colours and size to suit – a great blanket for a partner, pet or fresh baby, I think!

<u>YOU NEED</u>:

×   ODDMENTS OF YARN OR AROUND 12 × 50G BALLS OF YARN (I USE DK)

×   A 3.5MM CROCHET HOOK

×   YARN NEEDLE WITH A LARGE EYE

×   SCISSORS

×   SOMETHING NICE ON THE TELLY

<u>LET'S MAKE IT</u>:

1.   Chain 63.

2.   Skip the first stitch. Treble once into each stitch until the end of the row.

3.   Chain two and turn. Treble once into the back loop of each stitch in the row below. Each stitch has two loops – you only want to crochet through the back one. Do this all the way along the row, then chain two and turn.

4.   Repeat until you have 12 rows. They'll be lovely and textured and neat. Go you!

5.   Make 24 rectangles. Sew them into rows of three with neat whip-stitches. Then sew these rows together, matching joins and edges neatly. Weave in any loose threads with a yarn needle.

6.   Marvel at your gorgeous work and get cosy!

NB: You could make this in three strips and change colour as you go – but I like the hand-sewn, patchy effect of having individual rectangles!

FIVE-FINGER DISCOUNT KNITTED POMPOM SCARF

These instructions look complex, but this is super-easy and heaps of fun to make! If you get a bit stuck, YouTube can help you with finger-knitting basics. This is the perfect crafternoon project, I think.

Some people just cannot be bothered to knit. They have neither the patience nor the inclination. This scarf is good for people like that, because it only takes a couple of hours from start to finish. And it's good for knitters, too, because it helps them wiggle their fingers in new, knitty, non-needley ways! Finger-knitting for all, I say!

YOU NEED:

- × 2 × 50G BALLS OF BULKY (THICK!) YARN FOR THE SCARF
- × 2 × 50G BALLS OF REGULAR DK YARN FOR THE POMPOMS (SEE PAGE 175)
- × 2 PIECES OF THICKISH CARDBOARD (CEREAL PACKET!) EACH MEASURING ABOUT 15 CM × 15 CM
- × POMPOM TEMPLATE (SEE PAGE 177)
- × SCISSORS
- × FINGERS!

LET'S MAKE IT:

1. Find the loose end of each ball of wool and place them together. We're going to finger-knit two strands of yarn at once, to make a nice robust knit.

LET'S CAST ON!

1. With the back of your left hand facing you, drape the held-together strands of yarn over the back of that hand.
Be sure you have the loose yarn tail between your thumb and your forefinger. The loose tail should be around 20 cm long.

2. Turn your palm to face you, now, and clamp your thumb and forefinger together to hold the yarn in place. We're going to weave/wrap the yarn around our four fingers (not our thumb, though!) to create our first stitches.

3. Still keeping the yarn tail pinched firmly between your thumb and forefinger, begin to weave the yarn OVER your forefinger (keep pinching so your loose yarn doesn't come adrift), UNDER your middle finger, OVER your ring finger and then RIGHT AROUND your pinkie.

4. Now back across UNDER your ring finger, OVER your middle finger, RIGHT AROUND your forefinger.

5. Now UNDER your middle finger, OVER your ring finger and RIGHT AROUND your pinkie.

6. Now UNDER your ring finger, OVER your middle finger and UNDER your forefinger. Clamp the yarn (it's the thread attached to the ball of yarn) in between your thumb and forefinger to keep things secure.

7. Voila! You have cast on! Hurrah! Knitting Nancy you!

LET'S KNIT!

1. Let's begin knitting now by pulling our bottom loops over our top loops.

2. Always start at the pinkie when you are pulling your loops over. Use your right hand to lift the bottom loop up and over the top loop and set it free. You might need to bend your finger down a bit to make it work – that's just fine!

3. Move to the ring finger, lift the bottom loop up and over the top loop and set it free. Now do the same for the middle finger; bottom loop over top loop. And finally, lift the still-clamped loose yarn tail over the top loop as best you can, loosening your clamp if need be. Now set the loose yarn tail free, flinging it over the back of your work (away from the palm).

4. You will now have a loop on each of your four fingers.

5. Now we are going to weave/wrap another stitch onto each finger. Always starting with our forefinger for the weave/wrap, weave your yarn OVER the forefinger, UNDER the middle finger, OVER the ring finger and RIGHT AROUND the pinkie. Then UNDER the ring finger, OVER the middle finger and UNDER the forefinger, clamping your yarn between the forefinger and the thumb once more to keep it secure.

6. Now, starting at the pinkie, pull the bottom loops over the top loops one finger at a time. Next wrap the yarn over the forefinger, under the middle finger, over the ring finger, around the pinkie and under the ring finger, over the middle finger and under the forefinger.

7. Continue on like this, pulling the bottom loops over the top loops starting at the pinkie side of your hand until you have only one loop on each finger. Then weave/wrap the yarn over and under (as described above) beginning with over your forefinger, under, over, around your pinkie. Then weaving under, over, under back to your forefinger.

8. This pattern continues until your scarf is as long as you want it to be! If you need to set your work aside, just loosen your stitches from your hand and slide a pencil or knitting needle through them to keep them safe. Be sure to tie a piece of yarn at the pinkie end, so you don't put your stitches back on the wrong fingers!

9. Here's how to finish your scarf off. Lift the loop off your pinkie and onto the ring finger. Now pull the bottom loop up over the top loop on your ring finger and set it free. Next, lift the loop which remains on your ring finger onto your middle finger. Pull the bottom loop over the top loop and set it free. Lift the loop on your middle finger off and onto your forefinger.

10. Now lift the bottom loop over the top loop and set it free. You have just one loop left now! Cut your yarn to form a longish tail (about 20 cm) and remove the final loop from your finger. Pull the loose yarn through this loop and pull tight to fasten off.

Attach the pompoms:

11. Make your pompoms and then attach them to the ends of your scarf by threading the loose yarn tail through your wool needle. Stitch it firmly into place using lots of small stitches. Use the yarn needle to weave in any loose yarn tails from your scarf, too, weaving the needle in and out of the scarf stitches a few times and then snipping the tail close to your work.

ART ATTACK ABSTRACT PAINTING

I love colour and I love making things and I love shapes. A blank canvas is the perfect focus for all this love. Perhaps you'd like to dip your brush in some paint too?

For my painting, I thought about the kinds of things I liked as a child. I liked collecting things, pretty colours, treasures and beachcombing. I started painting with this in mind, mixing the colours until they were the hue I wanted and painting all kinds of shapes as I hummed along.

YOU NEED:

×   CHEAP ($3!) TUBES OF ACRYLIC PAINTS IN PRIMARY
    COLOURS, PLUS SEVERAL TUBES OF WHITE PAINT TO MIX
    THINGS UP A BIT

×   PAINTBRUSHES IN VARIOUS SIZES
    (I USED DISCOUNT STORE ONES)

×   A CANVAS FROM THE DISCOUNT STORE (THESE ARE READY
    TO PAINT ON)

×   PAPER OR PLASTIC PLATES FOR MIXING COLOURS ON

×   A BIG JAR FULL OF WATER TO KEEP YOUR BRUSHES WET/CLEAN

×   AN OLD TOWEL TO CLEAN UP YOURSELF/SPILLS

LET'S MAKE IT:

1. Squeeze a bit of paint onto the paper plate. Add your mixing colour bit by bit, going slowly, until you have a shade you like. You might need to add some white or a bit more base colour if you go too light or too dark. Play around and have fun with it.

2. You can make your painting look like mine, mixing pastel colours and brushing them on. Or perhaps you want to

do something different? Maybe thin the paint down a bit (just add water) and plop it on to the canvas with a spoon? Keep it thick and trawl through it with a fork? Make it runny and squeeze it on with a squeezy bottle? Slather on some texture with a painter's spatula or plastic knife? The sky is the limit.

3.   If you don't like the results, wipe off as much as you can with an old towel and let it dry. Then paint it white and start again.

'YOUR BEST ANGLE' BROOCH

These take no time to make and are really satisfying to whip up. This amount of balsa wood makes 20 brooches at least – you could make one for every outfit or get crafting for your friends!

YOU NEED:

- × 1 SMALL PLANK OF 5MM-THICK BALSA WOOD (MINE WAS 1M × 9.15CM)
- × A CUTTING MAT
- × A SHARP STANLEY KNIFE
- × A METAL RULER
- × ACRYLIC PAINTS (I USED CHEAP STUDENT PAINTS)
- × A SMALL PAINTBRUSH
- × MASKING TAPE
- × BROOCH BACKS
- × SUPERGLUE

LET'S MAKE IT:

1. Use your Stanley knife and ruler to very carefully (please don't hurt yourself!) cut your balsa wood into triangle shapes. The triangles don't have to be perfect or equilateral unless you are a total geometry nut. They can be the same basic triangle shape, or you can go a bit wild. You could even make other shapes, if you're super-fancy.

2. Once you've cut all your shapes out, you need to get them ready to paint. Take your masking tape and apply tape to the triangle shape, so that the edge of the tape creates a 'border' for your blocks of paint.

3. Paint your triangles in the colours you like. Allow to dry.

4. Then flip them over and glue the brooch backs neatly into place. Don't glue your fingers. Try to keep the brooch back nice and straight and avoid getting glue on the closing/opening mechanism.

5. Ta-dah! You're done! Gift them to rad people!

FIRM FRIENDS NECKLACE

I used to make more brightly coloured versions of these in art class at primary school. Get fashiony and make these for all your favourite people!

YOU NEED:

× POLYMER CLAY LIKE SCULPEY OR FIMO IN YOUR CHOSEN COLOUR AND WHITE

× A METAL OR WOODEN SKEWER

× A LENGTH OF LEATHER THONGING OR RIBBON

× AN OVEN

× A CLEAN HEATPROOF PLATE OR BAKING TRAY

LET'S MAKE IT:

1. Preheat your oven to 130°C.
2. Start by mixing your colours, one by one. I used pink, so first I rolled a bead into a ball using the pink straight from the packet. I tried to make the ball as neat as possible.
3. Then use the skewer to put a hole in the bead, big enough for threading. The best way to make the hole is to gently 'drill' the skewer into the clay, twisting it around and around so it doesn't squish your bead out of shape.
4. I took another, smaller bit of pink clay and kneaded a little bit of white clay into it. Once it was well combined, I rolled another ball and skewered a hole in it as before.
5. Continue on making your beads in lighter and lighter shades and making holes big enough for threading.
6. Once your beads are all done, put them on the plate and into the oven for 20 minutes to harden.
7. Then, thread them onto your thonging or ribbon and tie a knot to secure the ends.
8. Voila!

EIGHTIES ARM-CANDY SAFETY-PIN BRACELET

In the eighties, my friend Yvonne and I used to make these bracelets all the time, wearing them snaking up our arms as we cracked our Hubba Bubba and thought about marrying all of Duran Duran. (I swear we thought we'd grow up and become Vivienne Westwood.)

YOU NEED:

× 54 SAFETY PINS (I USED SIZE 2 — THEY'RE 1½ INCHES LONG)

× 1M OF QUALITY SILVER ELASTIC CORD (AS THIN AS POSSIBLE TO FIT THROUGH THE SAFETY PINS NICELY)

× AROUND 50G OF SEED BEADS IN COLOURS YOU LIKE (THEY NEED TO BE AT LEAST SIZE 6 TO FIT ON THE SAFETY PINS NICELY)

× SCISSORS

LET'S MAKE IT:

1. Thread the beads onto the open (spiky) safety pin. Be careful not to poke yourself! Snap the pin closed when you've filled it with beads: you can thread them on randomly or make a pattern. Have a play and see what looks good to you!

2. Cut two 25 cm lengths of elastic. One is for the top of the bracelet and one is for the bottom.

3. Once you've filled all 54 pins with beads, thread the elastic through the hole in the TOP of each pin. Make sure all your beaded pins are facing the same way, and thread them onto the elastic one by one.

4. Once they're all threaded onto the first length of elastic, try it on for size. You might want to add more pins or take some out if it's too big. Then pull the elastic firmly, but not tight. Knot the elastic two or three times to secure and jiggle the knot between the pins and out of sight.

5. Now thread the elastic through the bottom of the pins in the same way. Tie it off firmly and securely once you're done.

6. Shimmy the bracelet onto your arm and fist bump your favourite people in style!

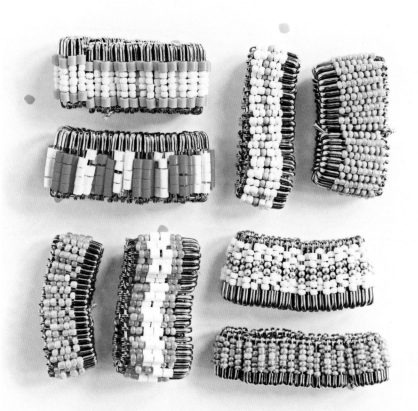

SPARKLY PONY MOBILE

I made this in cute pastel colours, but you could go wild with bold colours or deep neutrals and metallics for more sophisticated sparkles. This is the perfect project/gift for the young and young-at-heart. Who doesn't love a sparkly pony?

YOU NEED:

- × ONE EMBROIDERY HOOP (OURS MEASURED 25CM IN DIAMETER)

- × 20M OF PRETTY RIBBON IN COLOURS YOU LIKE

- × 3.5M OF WHITE RIBBON TO HANG THE PONIES FROM

- × 4 SQUARES OF FELT (I USED WHITE)

- × THREAD (CHOOSE A COLOUR TO MATCH THE FELT)

- × SKEINS OF EMBROIDERY FLOSS IN PRETTY COLOURS FOR THE PONIES' MANE AND TAIL, AND TO HANG YOUR MOBILE BITS AND BOBS (6 SKEINS IS PLENTY!)

- × PLAIN PAPER AND A PEN

- × STUFFING

- × BLACK EMBROIDERY FLOSS FOR THE PONIES' EYES

- × BEADS FOR THE HANGING THREADS (I USED ABOUT 50 IN VARYING SIZES)

- × SEED BEADS TO DECORATE THE PONIES' BACKS IN A FEW CUTE COLOURS

- × ABOUT 20 INDIVIDUAL SEQUINS IN CUTE COLOURS FOR SPARKLY PONY BACKS

- × SCISSORS

- × PINS

- × NEEDLE

- × BEADING NEEDLE (TO FIT THROUGH THE MIDDLE OF LITTLE SEED BEADS)

LET'S MAKE IT:

1. Draw a pony shape onto a sheet of paper.
2. Fold a felt square in half. Pin your pony template to the felt and cut out a matching pair of ponies. (These two pieces will be sewn together later to form one 3D pony!)

3. Sew on the sequins and beads in a cute random formation. I sewed mine to just one side of the pony (the one that faces outwards!), but you can stitch each of your pony's sides if you like.

4. Embroider the pony's eyes. I used a French knot.

5. Cut an 80 cm length of white ribbon. Cut some short lengths of embroidery floss for the tail and mane.

6. Lay one pony piece right-side down on your work surface. Position the mane and tail, and the length of ribbon extending out of the top of the pony's neck. Put the matching pony piece on top, right-side up, sandwiching the mane, tail and ribbon inside. Pin to secure.

7. Using matching thread, stitch from the pony's tummy almost all the way around the outside of the pony and back to the tummy, being sure to leave a gap for stuffing. Stuff with tiny pieces of toy stuffing and then stitch closed with matching thread.

8. Repeat the process, making three more ponies, attaching their tails, manes and hanging ribbons as you go.

9. Cut a 1 metre length of embroidery floss, tie a knot in one end and thread your beads onto them. Make four lengths like this.

10. Separate the embroidery hoops by unscrewing the closure. Tie your ponies and beads to the smaller (inside) hoop.

11. Tie lengths of embroidery floss to the outer hoop at regular intervals. Tie these lengths together to form a hanging point.

12. Next, carefully drape lengths of ribbon over the inside hoop. I used 60 cm lengths, but you can make yours longer or shorter, whatever looks good to you.

13. Being careful to not let the ribbons slip off (ask a friend to help!), place the outer hoop over the inner hoop, catching the ribbons (but not the hanging point) inside. Screw closed.

14. Pick up your mobile by the hanging point. Attach a length of floss or string at the point where all four strands meet. Hang in your favourite spot and marvel at your pretty ponies!

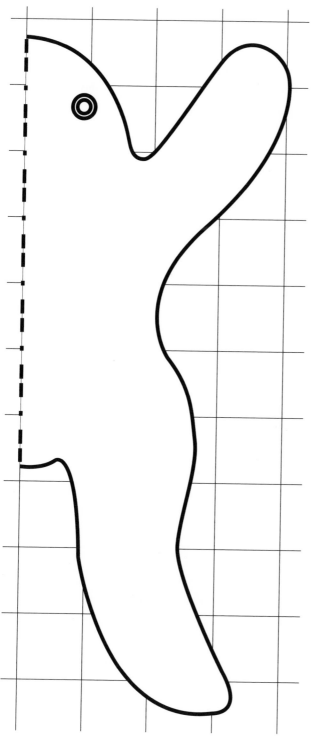

FROG TEMPLATE

ENLARGE
BY 30%

FLORAL FROG

This project reminds me of lovely things about my childhood: Liberty prints, beanbag toys, slimy-but-cute pets and *Sesame Street*. Make a whole bunch for your friends or sew a stack for home!

YOU NEED:

× A FAT QUARTER OF FABRIC (I USED LIBERTY!)

× SOME RICE TO FILL YOUR FROG

× SEWING MACHINE WITH THREAD TO MATCH YOUR FABRIC

× SCISSORS

× NEEDLE AND THREAD

× PINS

× FROG TEMPLATES × 2 (SEE PAGE 199)

× AN IRON

× A CHOPSTICK OR KNITTING NEEDLE

× A FUNNEL

LET'S MAKE IT:

1. Press your fat quarter of fabric nicely with a hot iron. Fold it in half (width-ways) and press on the fold to make a neat line.

2. Now unfold it again. Using the pressed-in line as a guide, fold one edge in to meet that line. Press. Fold the other edge in to meet the same line. Press. You now have a fat quarter with both edges folded into the centre and neatly pressed.

3. Pin your frog template to one folded edge. Pin the other frog template to the other folded edge. You're pinning through two layers of fabric.

4. Carefully cut your frogs out, being careful not to cut the folded edge (or you will be cutting your frog in half!). Unpin your two frogs and set the templates aside for another day.

5. With right sides facing, pin your fabric frog shapes together.

6. Starting at the top of one leg, sew down the leg and all the way around the frog until you reach the other leg. Sew up the other leg, leaving a gap between froggy's legs for stuffing. Sew around the frog a second time for extra strength (still leaving the gap for stuffing).

7. Trim the seams and loose threads and turn the frog the right way out, pushing any stubborn bits gently with a chopstick or knitting needle to make sure you have a neat frog shape.

8. Use the funnel to syphon the rice into your cute frog. Don't fill it up too much, but enough to give it a good shape. Sew it closed neatly, tucking in any raw edges and keeping your stitches as tiny as possible.

REFERENCES

CHAPTER THREE

→ Joseph Stromberg, 'A week of camping can turn you into a morning person', Smithsonian.com, 2 August 2013.

→ Natasha Turner, 'Five health benefits of vitamin D that might surprise you', Chatelaine, 2 May 2013.

→ Julie Chao, 'More fresh air in classrooms means fewer absences', Berkeley Lab, 5 June 2013.

→ 'Five ways to be more creative', BBC Science, 13 March 2013.

CHAPTER FOUR

→ Leo Babauta, 'The fear of being found a fraud', Zen Habits, 8 August 2013.

CHAPTER FIVE

→ Hailey Bartholomew, 'Picket fenced-in', vimeo.com/13998609.

→ Amy Krouse Rosenthal, '17 things I made', youtube.com/watch?v=o3eZvEIdmq4.

CHAPTER SIX

→ 'Five ways to be more creative', BBC Science, 13 March 2013.

CHAPTER EIGHT

→ Peter Miller, 'Twins', *National Geographic*, January 2012.

CHAPTER TEN

→ Marilynn Marchione, 'Retiring later may help prevent dementia, study finds', The Huffington Post, 15 July 2013.

→ Lauren Turner, 'How retirement can seriously damage your health', *The Independent*, 16 May 2013.

THANK YOUS

Thanks so much to my family:
Cam, Max, Rin, Ari, Joe, Sara, Andy,
Mum, Sean, Nan, Mason, Zoe.

Thanks to my sweet friends
for their general ace-ness.

Thanks to the people who read my blog
for their encouragement.

Thanks to the creative people who gave
me little pushes along the way.

VIKING

UK | USA | Canada | Ireland | Australia
India | New Zealand | South Africa | China

Penguin Books is part of the Penguin Random House group of companies
whose addresses can be found at global.penguinrandomhouse.com.

Penguin
Random House
Australia

First published by Penguin Group (Australia), 2015

1 3 5 7 9 10 8 6 4 2

Cover and text design by Ortolan
Illustrations Kat Macleod and Ortolan
Photographs by Julie Renouf
Styled by Michelle Mackintosh
Animal and badge collages by Pip Lincolne
Typeset in Garamond Premier Pro by Samantha Jayaweera © Penguin Group (Australia)
Printed and bound by Hung Hing, China

National Library of Australia
Cataloguing-in-Publication data:

Craft for the soul: how to get the most out of your creative life / Pip Lincolne.
9780670076598 (paperback)
Creative ability. Creative thinking. Inspiration.
Creation (Literary, artistic, etc.)

153.3

penguin.com.au